10p

D1436498

UNDER A LILAC-BLEEDING STAR

LESLEY BLANCH

UNDER A
LILAC-BLEEDING STAR

Travels and Travellers

JOHN MURRAY

Printed in Great Britain for
John Murray Albemarle Street London
by William Clowes & Sons Limited
London & Beccles

For
MARK RAGAN BAUTZER,
in his new world—something
about my old one

Contents

Illustrations

[1] Photo: Roger Viollet
[2] Copyright Paul Popper Ltd.
[3] Photo: C. Sfetea
[4] Photo: John Hillyard
[5] By courtesy of the Ashmolean Museum

Acknowledgements

I wish to thank the Editors of the following publications in which some of my pieces have previously appeared: The *Cornhill Magazine*, *Picture Post*, *Harpers Bazaar*, *Show Magazine*, the *Observer*, the *Reporter*, the *Leader*, *Vogue Magazine*, The Condé Nast Publications, *Holiday*.

Acknowledgement should also be made to Cassell and Co. Ltd. who published *The Story of My Life* by Queen Marie of Roumania.

I am particularly indebted to Mr. Malcolm Josceline Nicolson's notes and unpublished biography of his mother, which, by his courtesy I was allowed to see.

Author's Note

In the Balkans the peasants say that if you long for faraway countries and leave your own land and home to find them, you are born under A LILAC-BLEEDING STAR.

Perpetuam Mobile

Only an astronaut's voyage could have satisfied that fervent band of women travellers who were a peculiar manifestation of the nineteenth century. Neither before nor since have any voyagers approached travel with quite the same enthusiasm for mileage. Although the ladies recorded their journeys in detail, we do not sense so much their interest in the goal as the distances covered. In some cases their lives became a *perpetuam mobile*. The habit of movement, of ever-changing horizons, had infected them. There was no cure. They could not come to a standstill anywhere, either in the homes they had left or in the regions they obtained, and they were forever off again, whirling round the globe like tops (or astronauts), their skirts and petticoats billowing round them as they spun onwards; a fabulous giddy-go-round. In their journals they record their mileage with the exactitude and total absorption which hypochondriacs reserve for their pulse or temperature, and we see that it becomes a positive point of honour with them to add another two or three thousand miles to any itinerary.

Mostly they went alone; sometimes they dragged a husband along; seldom, if ever, a lover, for nothing is so destructive to a love-affair as constant gaddings, packing and unpacking, and the distraction of the scenery; to say nothing of admirers encountered en route. Occasionally the ladies seemed to believe they were following, or accompanying, a husband, as in the case of Madame Hommaire de Hell, who recorded her husband's geological findings; or Sir Richard Burton's wife, who lived by his celebrated dictum: *pay, pack and follow*—all over the world. But no man was ever so intoxicated with distance for its own sake as this band of women.

Perhaps it was the cumulative effect of so many centuries of domesticity which fired them. In the nineteenth century keeping house had reached crushing proportions morally, socially and physically. True, for the average household there was no shortage of servants: but never had there been so many children, relatives, rooms or guests either. Never were women so chained. Every moral and legal code obliged them to live narrowly restricted lives. European or Western women, that is; in the Orient it was at once better and worse. Perhaps that too influenced the lady travellers. Perhaps those few who escaped, enjoyed not so much the darkling glances of foreign men, as the sight of their even more restricted Eastern sisters. After an invitation to visit the harem or a glimpse of purdah, it is probable that the massive mahogany confines of the Western nineteenth-century home appeared less irksome. Though perhaps not: for while the divans of the harem hinted unimaginable delights, the double-bed upstairs seemed consecrated to breeding. In any case, for the travelling ladies, home was the last place where the heart was.

✣   ✣   ✣

A young Frenchwoman, Lise Cristiani, is the perfect example of this type: a curious girl who came to sublimate both her brilliant career as a violinist and her personal life as a woman to the chimera of distance. Let us follow the comic overtones of her essentially tragic, and brief, life. She first appears in Paris, in the 1840's, as a fragile-looking girl with large soft, dark eyes and a pale face framed in ringlets. She had been a child prodigy and her technical mastery was matched by her interpretative quality. When first she set out to conquer other worlds she had no doubt been led abroad by dreams of purely professional ambition. No thoughts then of distance for distance's sake. She had won Copenhagen overnight. The snug little city, with its splendid formal palace, its precise parks, and ships' masts piercing the chill skies between the chimney-pots clustered along the canals and harbours, was very different from the sprawling, careless grandeur of Paris; but its audiences were all she could ask. In recognition of her talents she was appointed *violoniste du Roi*. Next, the Swedes welcomed her, and in Stockholm she was known as the *Sainte Cécile Française*. She began to eye further horizons.

Soon after her twentieth birthday she was engaged for a concert tour in the principal cities of Russia. Russia! Snowy steppes—wolves—grand dukes; Count Razoumovski, Beethoven's patron, had been Russian. Russian audiences were celebrated for their musical enthusiasm. The prospect enchanted her. All the leading musicians of Europe returned from Russia with glowing accounts of their reception. Indeed, when Liszt had disapproved of the Tzar Nicholas I talking loudly through his recital, he had firmly shut the piano, saying: 'Music itself is silent when Nicholas speaks.' And the audience's reaction, though understandably uneasy at such audacity, had been most gratifyingly on the artist's side. Mademoiselle Cristiani set out with perfect confidence, an old German pianist as accompanist beside her. But on reaching St. Petersburg, she met the first check in her career. A member of the Tzar's family had died suddenly; the Court was plunged into mourning and her most powerful patrons compelled to languish beside their own hearths. Her recitals were cancelled. The impresarios and concert-hall managers shrugged off their losses. It was God's will, they said, displaying that Slav acceptance of fate which so closely approximates to Arab fatalism. *Mektoub!* or *Nietchievo!* are both expressions of passivity.

For Mademoiselle Cristiani there seemed no other course than to accept fate and return to France. But she had already taken the first step which led her to that passion for far distances. She had already travelled five thousand miles—why not another five thousand? Already the strange germ of mileage had taken hold. She would go on. If the Russian capital was closed to her, she would take herself further afield—east, to those Asiatic Siberian territories of which she had heard so much while in St. Petersburg. They were the latest, largest developments of the great thrusting country. There, she believed, she would find appreciative audiences, unshadowed by any considerations of Imperial grief. Siberia was then beginning to be envisaged in terms of colonial expansion, a rich field for agriculture and trade, besides the fabulous resources of the mines, which exploited convict labour. Irkutsk, the capital, was a prosperous place, building its university and opera house, and it was here that the Governor-General lived in state. The dread convict settlements were further afield. As the small towns sprang up, some of their most respected new citizens were first and second generation descendants of the earlier political exiles who had, when faced with appalling difficulties, retained a cultivated milieu. Everything Mademoiselle Cristiani heard of Siberia convinced her that her musicianship would be properly appreciated there. And, en route, there would be eager audiences in Tobolsk, Omsk and Tomsk. . . . Three thousand miles of unknown distances to conquer! The first stirrings of her strange craving had now crystallized.

She started east, in a bone-shaking *telega*, a wooden vehicle generally used for long journeys. With her went a Russian maid and the old German accompanist. 'I practise assiduously, en route, for I know how much will be expected of me,' wrote the musician; while the woman wrote: 'Natasha is a real necessity on such a journey. I rely on her to look after my clothes: everything is covered in dust, or sadly crumpled, I arrive looking like a scarecrow.' But the traveller, as yet unacknowledged, remained silent before the intoxicating realities of this three-thousand-mile journey. While the old German was charged with the care of her violin, cradling it in

4

his arms, to protect it from the jarring, pitching motion of the *telega*, Lise Cristiani sat staring around her avidly.

They drove east—ever further into the nomad steppes, and each day the Asiatic landscape grew more sinister, even more sparsely inhabited, more foreboding. Gradually the difficulties of obtaining a night's lodging came to occupy all their thoughts. They followed the posting road, but even so the wayside inns grew fewer. They drove on, often sleeping where they changed horses, at primitive *stancais*, vermin-infested wayside shacks, or the *étapes*, military-controlled halts designed for the trudging lines of convicts, men, women and children, political exiles and felons, dragging their chains on the cruel stages of a forced march which often took them years to accomplish. Each night, stiff with fatigue, Lise Cristiani's little party would climb down from their *telega* and, half-frozen, stagger into whatever shelter they had reached.

Beside the stove, and surrounded by wondering peasants, a handful of Cossack guards, or even some wretched convoy of prisoners, the violinist stubbornly continued to practise her roulades and cadenzas. There being no pianos in such surroundings, the old accompanist dozed and snored, waking fitfully to beat time, and snore again, while Natasha, hunched over her sewing, repairing the torn hems, broken stay-laces, or bedraggled bonnet-strings of her young mistress—a daily toll exacted by such a journey, but no longer strictly necessary, since appearances were becoming of less and less importance.

At last, arrived in Irkutsk, they found the city at once more primitive, and even more appreciative, than they had imagined. It had none of the architectural beauties of mediaeval Tobolsk; no golden-domed cathedrals or splendid kremlins. The unpaved streets sprawled across empty acres of mud. The rough wooden houses that lined them stood back behind high fences; puddles stretched across the streets and were often knee-deep pools into which household refuse was flung. There was no street lighting, few shops, only one weekly newspaper, a handful of fly-blown restaurants or frowzy commercial hotels, and a doubtful-looking pharmacy. But many of the well-to-do merchants were late-comers, who treasured a certain cultural heritage from their life in Moscow and St. Petersburg. Some of the settlers were those political exiles known as Dekabrists—the flower of Russia's aristocratic and cultured élite. And the Russians, from moujiks to the military garrison, were a passionately musical people.

So unusual a visitor as the celebrated young French musician intrigued the people of Irkutsk and all walks of life welcomed her. General Mouraviev, the Governor-General, was particularly hospitable, removing her from the shortcomings of the Grand Hotel du Commerce, inviting her to his official residence, a large, classical white building overlooking the wide waters of the Angara, where he lived in princely state. Today it is the library of the city of Irkutsk, and when I was there, the chief Librarian showed me some of its treasures. But I found myself eyeing the chandeliers and the elaborate white porcelain stoves with more interest, wondering if they were the same as in Lise Cristiani's day. She speaks of a certain absence of the more accepted Western comforts, but there was such an overlay of splendours (solid silver chamber-pots screened by hangings of gigantic white bearskins) that the young Frenchwoman was enthralled by the exotic turn her life had taken. Here she was, in a palace in Siberia, supping on caviar, tuning up her violin to play to dashing Cossack officers who could discuss the niceties of a Mozart quartet as knowledgeably as the latest type of rifle. Her host was an outstanding figure of his day. He had lately realized his dreams of Russia's colonial expansion along the Chinese borders of the Amur River. Moreover, he had accomplished this coup without bloodshed and was the hero of the hour, both in Irkutsk and St. Petersburg. His monument, unlike many Tzarist heroes, has never been removed from its place of honour and still dominates the public gardens: and here, once again, I found Lise Cristiani

6

dominating my thoughts, so that I saw the kind, moustachioed face on the monument as her host rather than the great administrator.

Mouraviev immediately arranged that his visitor should give a series of recitals, first in Irkutsk, and then in some of the less remote provincial towns, such as Yeniseisk—centre of the convict settlements, where, we may imagine the plaintive tones of her violin floating out across the twenty-foot-high wooden stockades of the prisons, brought a melancholy joy to the forgotten beings who dragged their fetters round the prison yard, as they took their brief daily airing.

When the Governor-General left Irkutsk on an official mission to Kiakhta, on the Chinese frontier, Mademoiselle Cristiani accompanied him. From there she had made up her mind to push on—further east. 'I shall play everywhere—in Pekin, even', she wrote to her anxious family in Paris. Kiakhta was only about a thousand miles from Pekin. True, the dreaded Gobi Desert lay between, but she felt no qualms. By now her passion for movement—for distance—had taken form. The further and wilder her destination, the better she was pleased. It is doubtful, had Pekin been only a day's posting from Irkutsk, if she would have felt such a surge of enthusiasm. But the doubly alluring prospect of playing to Chinese audiences and journeying yet another thousand miles to do so, was positively intoxicating. She saw herself travelling in a box-litter of Chinese fashion, scarlet lacquer, and carried by coolies. Under burning suns, they were following camel trains crossing the Gobi wastes; but neither thirst, nor the serpents that abound there, nor yet the bleached bones of less fortunate travellers, could turn them back.

Already she saw herself installed in some jade pavilion of the Summer Palace, executing a Paganini Étude with such brilliance, that the impassive yellow faces of her Manchu audiences broke at last into smiles of rapturous enthusiasm. Alas, while still at Kiakhta, and still under Mouraviev's protection, she discovered the drawbacks of being a European woman on the edge of outer Mongolia.

Kiakhta was divided in two by a broad esplanade. Russians lived on one side, Chinese on the other. The two sections of the community seldom met. It was a merchant population, the centre of the tea trade, with yak caravans, camels and men converging there with tin-lined boxes of merchandise. After a good deal of manoeuvring, she managed to obtain an invitation to dinner from the Chinese; but it was a formal, all-masculine affair, a gesture of Asiatic *politesse*, no more. With the last bows and ceremonial leave-takings, she was once again back among the provincial Russians, and she had not been invited to play, either after dinner or in Pekin. The Chinese had found a way to snub Mouraviev and the Russians, through their French protégée.

✤   ✤   ✤

However, all the rest of Asia lay ahead. Mademoiselle Cristiani was not to be discouraged. Leaving the sheltering Mouraviev wing, she set out to visit the Buriat-Mongolian camps, playing Bach and Bellini to them in return for a night's lodging in their round felt-covered huts or *yurts*. Buriat tribes had been under Cossack domination for a century or more and now knew better than to question any personage arriving from Russia. Their inscrutable flat faces showed neither surprise nor pleasure when she appeared among them. She was travelling with an escort of Cossacks, supplied by Mouraviev, so they bowed her into their *yurts* and listened attentively.

Although to Asiatic ears the music she played must have sounded incomprehensible, she appears to have possessed some potent magic, for, wherever she went, both civilized audiences and intractable savages fell under the spell of her playing. There is no means, today, of measuring her standing, musically; it would seem that by nature of her many engagements in the capitals of Europe she was of the front rank. That, at last, her musical career was sacrificed to far distances was eloquent of the strength of her passion. Health, professional prestige, personal life, all were sacrificed to this exacting god of mileage. She who had once known the applause of Europe's *cognoscenti* was now lured on, first, by the thought that she would be travelling into a further horizon for her next recital.

✢   ✢   ✢

In an overcrowded *yurt* the Buriats cannot have been an altogether agreeable audience. They were a nomadic people who passed for the dirtiest race in all Asia, their sheepskin coats swarmed with lice and their tallowy skins reeked of sweat. But Lise Cristiani makes no mention of their short-comings. She was seven thousand miles from the Salle Pleyel and found this rewarding enough. By now the maid Natasha and the old accompanist had dropped by the way, or been cast aside like the excess baggage they had become. No Buriat-Mongolian *yurt* possessed a piano, nor was there any more need to keep up concert-hall appearances—even though there were occasional visits to the larger lamaseries, which counted as social events.

At Guisinoi Ozera, three hundred miles out of Irkutsk, the great whitewashed monastery with its red and gold roofed temples flung open its doors to her and the orange robed monks led her in state to play before the Grand Lama. He received her ceremoniously, seated on a scarlet throne piled with saffron cushions, and, offering ritualistic little cups of tea, conversed through a merchant interpreter in a most worldly fashion. He spoke of Paris—which he believed to be an ungodly city; of the Tzar Nicholas I, 'a most mighty neighbour', he said enigmatically. When she offered to play for him, he graciously declined. 'After such a journey you must not exert yourself on my behalf,' he told her. '*My* musicians shall play for you instead.' Rising, he closed the interview by summoning a lesser lama to conduct her to the temple, where massed cymbals, drums, giant bronze trumpets and conch shells burst into a welcoming cacophony as she took her place.

From the Lamaserie the obsessed girl proceeded to explore the eastern shores of Lake Baïkal, 'the Holy Sea', the world's deepest fresh-water lake, where brilliant green sponges and monstrous-looking fish lurk, and the dark quartz cliffs over-shadow waters which rise suddenly and lash the lake into twenty-foot waves. Wandering along the lake's dramatic strand, crossing it in one of the frail bark canoes of the Buriats or camping among the fisherfolk, Lise Cristiani still clasped her violin, still believed she was returning, however circuitously, to France. But the pattern of her destiny was formed. She had reached the point of no return; and back in Irkutsk it was, in fact, no stopping-place on her journey homewards, but once more a starting-point.

When General Mouraviev lightly invited her, 'this crazy Frenchwoman', to accompany him on an official journey to Russia's northernmost port, Kamchatka, on the Bering Sea, he had not imagined she would accept. He had not gauged the degree of her mania. She accepted rapturously. 'I shall add yet another four thousand miles to my travels and thus complete my artist's life,' she wrote to her sadly anxious family in Paris.

In the romantic early years of the nineteenth century to speak of a woman 'completing her life' generally inferred she had taken a lover. (Later, entrenched in domesticity, the mid-Victorian woman's life was said to be 'ruined' by a lover and 'completed' by a numerous family.) But Lise Cristiani had made her own choice. For her completion was in terms of computation—miles, versts, leagues. . . .

✣   ✣   ✣

The Governor-General's party set out in great state with Cossack outriders, couriers, and wolfhounds. At night they still sped northwards, now bedded down in sable-lined, fur-covered sledges, the stars racing overhead, their way lit by the flaming torches of the outriders, great plumes of snow marking their progress as they cut through the deep white drifts. Heading for the Sea of Okhotsk, they travelled by way of the Amur provinces 'drawn by wild horses which had never known a harness', writes Mademoiselle Cristiani on a note of gratification, choosing, like most ardent travellers, local colour above comfort. At Okhotsk they embarked on a steamer bound for the Kamchatka Peninsula. The young violinist's siren songs (she was playing Scarlatti on deck) so captivated a whale that it sidled round and round the boat in a most alarming manner, and the Captain was obliged to put an end to the concert.

Kamchatka is the last outpost of Russian commerce, set down beside the frozen seas: it suffers fearful winters of fog and ice. But nothing discouraged the frustrated violinist. Although the late autumn was closing in, and the snows were already deep, her mania would not be stilled. Forward! Never mind where! The Governor-General became uneasy. He did not wish to be held responsible for such an obstinate guest. Finding all his warnings went unheeded, he at last withdrew his Cossack escort and turned back to Irkutsk, leaving Mademoiselle Cristiani alone. She had unfortunately learned that a government courier would shortly be leaving for Yakoutsk, in the interior, and was determined to accompany him. No matter that the snows had become exceptionally heavy, that the journey must be undertaken on horseback, under conditions of inconceivable hardship—she must go too. The route lay across the Stanovoi Mountains, crossing many frozen rivers: new territories—more mileage!

We can imagine this solitary figure, at once ridiculous and pathetic, still clasping her violin case, her agile fingers muffled in fur-lined gloves, her ringlets crammed beneath a hood of sea-otter fur as, trembling with cold and excitement, she met the courier's refusals by every argument and persuasion at her command.

The courier appears to have been an enigmatic and sullen young man, cold as his setting, impervious to the hardships of his metier, and unmoved by the French girl's blandishments. No doubt he had an orderly nature, liking everything in its rightful place and knowing that wayside huts of the frozen north were not the setting for dalliance, either musical or romantic. At last, exasperated by Mademoiselle Cristiani's insistence, he shrugged a bored acquiescence. So be it! They would start at daybreak, come what might.

In a dawn darkened by a gathering tempest, the dreaded *pourga*, this ill-assorted pair set out, mounted on the small, shaggy Mongolian ponies that alone can survive such conditions. In winter, when a calm spell has left the track between Okhotsk and Yakutsk fit for fast dog sledges, the journey can be done in little over two weeks' hard going: in such a period of snow-storms and blizzards as they now encountered, the journey might take well over a month, or it might end in a wayside death by freezing, as the courier pointed out with relish. But Lise Cristiani's mind was made up.

They left the low-lying frozen marshes of the coast for the taïga, scrub regions which stretched northwards to nothingness. Here, where only the bears and wild dog-packs lived, there were no villages, no settlements, only, sometimes, hunters' shelters, dilapidated wooden shacks already almost buried in snow, which the Siberian people contrived to keep furnished with a few strips of frozen meat, flint and fuel. This was a long tradition—as long as the prison settlements, as long as convicts had been escaping from them ... Few survived their wanderings, few were not hunted and shot down by the guards. 'A bullet always finds its runaway', says a Siberian proverb. Those who reached the taïga often lay hidden there for many months, snowed-up, as did the trappers who lost their way on hunting expeditions.

The frozen expanses they traversed revealed neither vegetation nor any trace of human life, and the *pourga* still howled round them. Sometimes they paused, more for the sake of the ponies than themselves, it seems; for there was no rest without warmth, and the courier seldom stopped long enough for a fire to be lit. They did not speak to each other. She was too proud to admit the pass to which her obstinacy had brought her, and no doubt far too exhausted to offer to play for him. She was now threatened with frost-bite, while snow-blindness with its agonizing pains went unalleviated. The courier did not bother to tell her of the local remedies—chewed tobacco poultices and such. He seems to have taken a sadistic pleasure in observing her increasing weakness and despair. After another week of black skies, under which the ponies inched their way, deep in snow-drifts, Lise Cristiani could stand no more. She begged for mercy—for one night's sleep in a hut, beside a fire. This was the courier's hour of triumph. He had not wished for her company. He was not interested in her as a woman, or as a musician. He had warned her of the dangers of such a journey, and he was unmoved, now, by her misery.

'I stop for no one. The Tzar's orders. En avant!' He cracked his whip and rode forward. He did not even look back at the wretched girl huddled in her inadequate pelisse. Now she was quite alone with those far distances she had craved so passionately. They were closing on her, freezing her with their icy breath, crushing her with the terrible intensity of their embrace. Now, suddenly, she knew herself betrayed. All the miles and versts and leagues had only led her towards death. . . . Their promises had been empty; they had demanded everything of her, and given nothing but a reckoning in return. The blizzard shrieked round her, seeming to taunt her soul, as it tormented her body. Her half-blinded eyes strained open to follow the courier's vanishing form. Another moment, and he would vanish into that dread white limbo-land. She must either follow him, or lie down and die. But her choice had been made long ago—she would remain true to her love, however cruel. She went on, winding the bridle round her numbed fingers, and crouching down over the pony's neck, passed into a coma, 'another dimension', as she described it, later, 'where only cold remained. It seemed as if my soul floated ice-bound before me, seeing that body which it could no longer inhabit or warm. . . .'

She survived this fearful journey, but her health was shattered. There were no more thoughts of violin recitals. As a concert artist, she had, not surprisingly, lost her touch. But as a traveller, she seemed content. 'I have just completed a journey of 18,000 miles,' she wrote home proudly. 'Fifteen Siberian towns, living among the Ostiks, Kirghiz and Kalmucks. . . . I have played where no artist has ever played before. I gave 140 concerts without counting private ones.' (Was the whale rated as a private or public audience, one wonders?) But later, she wrote bitterly: 'I know now that a rolling stone gathers no moss. . . . I have death in my soul.' The moss of security she had never craved, but she could not face immobility.

There seemed nowhere else to go, or at any rate, she had no more strength; she managed to crawl south to the Caucasus, where she hoped to regain her health but, quite soon after, she died at Novocherkassk, among the Don Cossacks. Cholera was raging there, and she succumbed almost overnight.

The population was touched by her youth and sad fate, and erected a handsome monument to her in the public gardens. Below the large stone cross lies a violin. 'The Artist's Other Soul', reads the inscription. But they should have inscribed her mileage: I think she would have chosen it as her epitaph.

2

God Rest Ye Merry Teddy Bear

I had given myself this journey as a Christmas present. For years I had promised myself the 'Golden Road to Samarcand' in my stocking. Now it was mine. I had spent a most unlikely Christmas Eve in Samarcand, once Tamerlaine's capital, and far from the rustle of gift-wrappings and all the commercial blackmail by which Christmas has come to be represented elsewhere, I had spent the day lolling on one of those large blue-painted wooden bedstead affairs that are set under the trees of every tchai-hana or tea-house of Central Asia. From this vantage point, and at the price of endless little bowls of green tea, I could watch the local population, Arabian night figures, in their striped khalats, a sort of padded dressing-gown, which, with an embroidered velvet skull-cap and high Russian boots, is the traditional costume of the Uzbek and Tadjik men of Turkestan. They were trotting to and from the bazaar on minuscule donkeys, or seated cross-legged in the white dust before their wares—grapes, home-made bird-cages of netted string, or little mounds of spinach-green powder, a kind of snuff they place under their tongues and savour voluptuously. Towards twilight, they crowded the tchai-hanas, lolling beside me, and like myself, contemplating, with a sort of ecstasy, the shimmering blue domes and minarets of this legendary city. Such an intense blue seems to grey-down even the cloudless Oriental skies.

Next morning, I flew on eastwards to Bokhara, another legendary and little-known city, where I had decided to spend Christmas day itself. I had not expected the little plane to come down, on so short a flight. But it did, quite suddenly, landing with a thump on the baked, cracked earth of a come-by-chance air strip on the edge of the Kizil Kum, or Red Sands, once the terror of every traveller or pilgrim crossing these deserts. Our pilot emerged from his cabin carrying a very large plush teddy bear, chocolate coloured and dressed in mauve check rompers, with a white collar fastened by a pink tulle bow. The navigator followed, lurching under the weight of a string bag stretched round several enormous tiger-striped melons. Both men were wearing a wide gold-toothed grin. 'Here we stopping one-two hours,' the pilot told me in English. He was a Tadjik, my neighbour, a Russian, said, watching him pitch down to earth without waiting for the steps which were now being hurtled towards us by two splendid creatures—again in the traditional khalat, now in chintz, printed in the most unlikely bunches of roses or blue and white flowers, but without effeminacy or sloppiness, when worn by such a virile race.

None of the other passengers, Uzbeks, Tadjiks, or a couple of Russian engineers (I was the only tourist) seemed surprised at this halt: but I had only just begun to realize the impromptu nature of local travel; impromptu, but not improvident. Mechanically, the planes and trains were highly efficient.

On the ground, a cold which belied the sun pierced through my sheepskin coat. I hurried towards the shelter of a small wooden hut topped by an aerial, the only sign of life. It was labelled, in Russian characters: KEEP OUT. One side was sheltered from the slicing wind and here I sat down gingerly, thinking about the vipers, monster scorpions, tarantulas and other disagreeable forms of insect life which flourish in these regions, and are not discouraged by cold. The navigator stacked the melons beside me and lay down to sleep, his head pillowed on their green gleaming flanks. The pilot, bowing with gallantry, now pressed the teddy bear into my arms.

'You will mind him out?' he asked, nearly colloquial. He

seemed in a great hurry to be gone and before I could reply, had flung himself into a decrepit jeep standing behind the hut. The jeep snorted and was off, bucking across the rough ground, dwindling into a dark speck as I watched its progress through spirals of red dust. All around lay limitless wastes, nothingness brought to its apogee in these dreaded deserts, Kizil Kum, the Red Sands, Kara Kum, the Black Sands, and Pak Bak Delli— the Steppes of Hunger to the Russian armies who took possession of the area a century ago.

Such was the strange country in which I now wandered, or rather, was dumped, on Christmas Day, a large teddy bear on my lap, and nothing to eat but a bag of caramels.

The noonday sun beat down strongly now, and the other passengers had joined the navigator in sleep. A young man in Western clothes (and very dull they seemed, after the chintzy khalats) emerged from the hut, and settled down beside me, producing a paper-back translation of *Room at the Top*. He was, he told me, the wireless operator, and studying industrial relations. I saw it would be useless to hope he might tell me any of the local legends of Nasr-e-din in Bokhara. It was very quiet, on the sunny side of the hut, but round the corner the wind whined and buffeted. The teddy bear and I sat staring out across Asia.

✣   ✣   ✣

During the years I had been collecting material for my book on the Caucasus, I had come across a great deal of extraneous, or as it were adjacent material. The Caucasus, the Crimea, the Turkoman Steppes, Uzbek territory, the Pamirs . . . moving east from the Moslem-held mountains of the Caucasus, all these regions merge, or abut, and the strange characters who peopled them, fought over them, or ventured into them all fascinated me so that I was perpetually side-tracked from my principal theme to follow the exploits of one or another, sharing, in my mind's eye the obsession of this Asiatic hinterland.

Now, at its most stark, it lay before me—the sanded, stony nothingness where countless caravans of merchants and pilgrims had perished. Few travellers, and until lately, no tourists had come this way. The Khans of Bokhara were celebrated for diabolic refinements of cruelty. 'Bokhara the Noble', so holy that light was said to *ascend* from it heavenwards, was also 'Bokhara the Terrible'. Beside the most sacred mosques in all Asia, lay the sinister fortress and palace of the Ark, where, between banquets and dalliance the emirs enjoyed watching the tortures to which their prisoners were put.

Until the end of the nineteenth century, to set out across these steppes was to walk towards death. Around 1830, three English officers had the temerity to try: their mission, to negotiate questions concerning the Afghan situation, border disputes and trade routes affecting the British position in India. Lieutenant Wyburd perished; so did Captain Connolly and Colonel Stoddart. Their slow end, imprisoned in 'the Black Well', their flesh gnawed off their bones by vermin especially reserved for such a purpose, is still a matter of ghoulish interest to the inhabitants of Bokhara. They were at last decapitated in the Reghistan, or square, before the Ark. The Emir, seated in state on a carpet-hung balcony, had watched the execution with particular relish, for the prisoners had refused his clemency at the price of abjuring Christianity. They were quite alone: no one could or would save them, in this faraway city. Both the Persian and Russian envoys to the Emir's Court had tried to temporize. But with their recall, there was no more help. The British Government, both in London and in the person of the Viceroy of India, had remained inexplicably inert.

Under a brazen June sky, the two skeletal and verminous figures were led out. Before the executioner's sword they embraced. 'We shall meet again soon, in heaven,' said

Connolly. They belonged to that small band of military mystics who were so remarkable a flowering of British arms during the nineteenth century, and of which we have particular examples among the officers of the Indian campaigns.

A year or two after the death of Connolly and Stoddart, the English public began to agitate—too late. At which the Reverend Joseph Wolff, a character of such excessive oddity that there is no space to do him justice here, set out for Bokhara, to determine the fate of his friend, Captain Connolly. Beneath the Reverend Joseph Wolff's canonicals (which he wore throughout the three months' journey) there beat a lion's heart. He stormed into the presence of the Emir, thundered his denouncements, quoted the Scriptures, demanded explanations, the bodies, threatened the might of Queen Victoria (who although a woman, was ever an awesome figure to Eastern potentates) and then, having suffered imprisonment and every threat, the parson was miraculously allowed to leave. He withdrew in majesty, his health impaired but his courage unshaken by this dreadful ordeal.

During the rest of the century there are very few records of other venturesome strangers making or surviving a visit to Bokhara the Terrible or crossing the Red Sands, the Black Sands, the Steppes of Hunger.

There were the dreaded wastes of which I had read, so often, in accounts of earlier, less pampered voyagers. Unlike myself, they had not been able to skim the wastes in a plane. They had plodded every parched or frozen mile, on camel or horseback. They knew the anguish of searching for water, of beating off raiding tribesmen or packs of wolves; or of surviving those fearful storms which skip across the desert in great spirals, hurling rocks before them like pebbles.

I remembered a local saying, something a shepherd had told me, in the foothills of the Pamirs: he had spoken arrogantly, as if proud of the harshness of his horizons. 'When creating the

World Allah made Baluchistan'—or was it not Bokhara?—
'from the refuse.'

Undoubtedly, nature is hostile here: man is plainly un-
welcome. What if the pilot did not return—if the radio
transmitter broke down? I glanced round me, furtively. The
wireless operator was dozing over *Room at the Top*; a solitary,
juicy looking horse-fly settled on the melons. The silence was
absolute. The sun was inclining rapidly, now, towards the
west: a chill crept up from the ground. It would not do to
think of nightfall. Clutching the teddy bear closer, I took
refuge in history, in that past which was still almost the present,
here in Central Asia.

✣   ✣   ✣

The Russians, expanding their vast empire eastward had
taken possession of the Turkoman steppes around 1862. The
Caucasus had fallen to them in 1854; the Amur provinces of
eastern Siberia, soon afterwards. The next acquisitions were
those Uzbek and Tadjik territories stretching between Tash-
kent, Samarcand and Bokhara. The fighting was violent and
soon done. One by one the conquered rulers, the khans and
emirs of each province settled back among their women and
their dancing boys, the adulated Batchas of Bokhara, soon
exchanging that inter-tribal warfare which had been their
pulse of life, for visits to St. Petersburg where they were
pampered guests of the Tzar. Their harems languished in
perfumed ennui, awaiting their overlords' return, but were
consoled by costly presents from the Tzar himself—Fabergé
opera glasses, for example. But what were they to watch, in
these wastes? Each other? Primitive puppet-shows, or the
peacocks screeching and strutting along the walls of the
harem? There were so few diversions. Presently, echoes of
civilization reached them, even there, at Khiva, Merv and
Ferganah, and they began sending for kid gloves and button

boots from Paris, while the khans ordered mechanical devices, cigar-cutters, musical boxes and shooting sticks, but all refulgently Oriental in style, damascened and studded with precious stones. The khans had now all become loyal vassals of the Great White Tzar. The Emir of Bokhara, with the aid of Russian engineers, constructed a railway line which, from Kokhand, served huge tracts of Central Asia and linked Siberia with the Caucasus. The four Khans of Merv stopped jockeying for power, imported a Russian physician and exchanged opium for champagne. Not to be outdone, the Khan of Khiva reduced his harem—said to be seven hundred strong—to a mere twenty.... Civilization had triumphed.

Only the people still sat in the bazaars, or under the trees, telling stories of Nasr-e-din, or crowded to pray in the great turquoise-tiled mosques, following the fanatic religious observances of their forefathers. And they whispered, still, of the cruelties and excesses of their rulers, the khans. True, the Russian Governor-General of Bokhara had suppressed the former practice of hurling criminals, trussed like fowls, from the highest minaret. It had been a popular diversion for the public, along with other kinds of public executions, by strangling, or slicing off the head. But still ... it smacked of barbarism. Only a handful of malefactors now rotted, chained, in the noxious city jails of Bokhara, and were flayed, starved, blinded or maimed, according to their crimes. But this, it was felt, was purely a question of local administration, something outside Tzarist Russia's sphere of influence. Thus the abuses continued until, with the Revolution in 1918, the last of the khans and emirs fled the Bolshevik troops, taking refuge across the neighbouring frontiers of Afghanistan or Iran. Since then, Bokhara the Noble, the Terrible, had declined steadily, till it became a ghost town where only a legend remained, where pure water had been piped in, but where the high walls of the city crumbled, and no travellers came and went through its nine great gates. This was the legend I had come to find, as I sat outside the wireless operator's hut, on the edge of the Kizil Kum.

✤ ✤ ✤

The stillness of the desert was abruptly broken by the noise of an approaching car. More spirals of red dust; then a rickety bus emerged, to disgorge half a dozen of the handsomest men I have ever seen. They were gigantic creatures, Uzbeks or Tadjiks, I could not distinguish, for all of them had the same traditional khalats, the same manner of walking like princes, their velvet-capped or turbanned heads held high, as they advanced on me, displaying the liveliest interest in both myself and the bear. They seemed to be expecting him, for he was seized and passed from hand to hand, approvingly. 'Tchoudessnie!' Wonderful, they said to me, in Russian. From behind the padded skirts of their khalats, I saw a very small girl peering at me fearfully. She was dressed in scarlet silk, with baggy trousers below her skirt. A number of tight little black braids were hanging from under her gold-embroidered pill-box cap. No doubt the bear was a long-promised toy. I held it out towards her.

'Yours?' I asked, in my basic Russian. But she backed away, shaking her head vehemently. She seemed anxious not to come too near such a fabulous creature. The splendid giants had now settled round me in a circle, sitting back on their heels in that curious upright, yet crouching, attitude seen in the early Persian miniatures. Their brown, beautifully shaped hands were tucked into their long rucked sleeves and their eagle-profiles were dark against the sky. I seemed to be as exotic a spectacle to them, as they were to me, and they plied me with questions in their halting Russian.

Why was I here? Where was my husband—home—children? Was it not a big celebration, today, among the Christians? A sort of Ramadan? Well, sort of, I conceded. Then why was I here? Why indeed? What makes a traveller? I felt my Russian was not up to so esoteric a subject, and I turned the conversation to their work—farming, cotton crops, houses—their families (I was careful not to enquire after their wives, knowing that Oriental etiquette forbids such mention), their climate, traditions, music even. . . . So I liked their music? Very much. Evidently my sincerity convinced them, for they began singing in chorus, swaying from side to side, beating their knees, and the ground, to accompany the harsh, staccato rhythms. Listening, entranced, I found myself beating time with the bear's stumpy arms. Goodwill overflowed all round. They laughed delightedly, the uncalculated laugh of children.

'Mischka likes our music', said one singer. (Bears are always called Mischka in Russia.)

Were there such bears in my country? asked the circle. Toy bears? Mischkas? Like this one? All at once I felt the tears come into my eyes. I remembered, so long ago, my own teddy bear, stuffed into my high-chair, sharing my mug of milk. . . . But now I was in Asia, a long long way from home.

'You love Mischka?' asked one of the crouched giants, plainly puzzled by my tears.

I nodded, feeling foolish, clasping the Tadjik teddy, looking down at his hind legs emerging stiffly from the check rompers. His round, velvet-lined ears and his smiling, trustful expression were the image of my nursery friend. Teddy bears have always seemed to me to be, above all other toys, the symbol of loving-kindness. Dolls can look mean. But no plush monkey, rabbit, or even dear Jumbo can ever achieve quite that degree of lovingness expressed by the teddy bear, wherever he is found.

I do not know the origin of the teddy bear, as a toy, but I believe it has some connection with a cub which Theodore 'Teddy' Roosevelt orphaned on a hunting expedition and then adopted as an *amende honorable*. The cub's furry charms were immortalized by an enterprising toy manufacturer, bringing joy to countless nurseries all over the world, for ever after.

God Rest Ye Merry Teddy Bear

Russian popular legends are full of stories of real live bears, who come from the forests, to play with the village children. There are many well-established cases of their tossing up crowing babies, catching them and cuffing them affectionately, like their own cubs. Those sad stories of a female bear being shot by hunters, who are afterwards pursued and savaged by the mate seem to me, not so much a proof of the animal's ferocity, as the strength of its love for its murdered mate. Russian and Balkan Gypsies, whose camps generally included tamed bears, often confided their babies to the bears, who would sit rocking them, held in their huge paws, with almost human devotion. Thus, it is not surprising that the teddy bear has come to symbolise affection—love.

There was a sudden stir among the Uzbeks; they were pointing across the desert to where the jeep was seen racing towards us. The giants sprang to their feet, like uncoiling steel springs; laughing and talking animatedly, they went to meet the jeep. The other passengers began to sit up, yawning. I remained where I was, the bear still on my lap, and the little girl staring at us from afar. The jeep hurtled to a stop and our pilot jumped out, shouting, as he rushed towards me. Seizing the teddy bear and the little girl, he kissed them both extravagantly. With some difficulty I now pieced together what everyone was trying to tell me. The pilot's wife had just given birth to a son, in a nearby village. She had been in labour when we left Samarcand and the pilot had broken the journey to be near her at this crucial hour. He had been counting on a son, and bought the teddy bear in anticipation, on his last visit to Moscow.

A son . . . a son deserved such a fine toy. The pilot, himself a Moslem, like all Tadjiks, shared the Oriental view of male offspring. To the East, daughters scarcely count. 'A girl-child is less use than a stone', runs a local proverb. 'With stones you can build a house. What use will a girl-child be?' But now the pilot had a son, and the little girl, who was his daughter, seemed forgiven for her shortcomings. Now we should proceed on our way, and the little girl would take the teddy bear back to her brother. She held it out to me, proudly, to say goodbye. I kissed its plushy snout.

✤   ✤   ✤

My mind drifted away from the Uzbeks, across the Steppes of Hunger, and all Turkestan, to another faraway scene, Sagamore Hill, on Long Island, once the Theodore Roosevelt family home. Now it is a museum, or memorial, left furnished as it was when they lived there. I had been spending one Christmas near by, at Oyster Bay, and on Christmas Eve we had driven over to join a straggle of tourists peering about the house. We had visited the lugubrious dining-room, seen the ample kitchens, climbed the stairs to the simply furnished attics, and followed the arrow to the lamp-lit drawing-room with its potted palms, frilly sofas and needlework baskets that Eleanor Roosevelt must have known when visiting there as a young bride. Outside, the raw winter dusk gathered, and the lamplight shone on the bare branches overhanging the house. Christmas carols were being relayed softly and incessantly through the house. It ought to have been corny, but it was curiously moving. Here was the echo of a home: a whole way of life that had been—and was gone . . . 'God Rest Ye Merry Gentlemen, Let Nothing Ye Dismay,' sang the disembodied choir as I followed the last sightseers to Theodore Roosevelt's library. It was a large, dark, masculine room, full of shiny leather armchairs, heavy desks and sporting trophies.

To give an added air of authenticity to the scene, the curators had arranged a large Christmas tree in the middle of the room. It was gaily decorated and underneath its frost-trimmed branches lay a pile of realistic-looking packages, gift-wrapped, as if awaiting the eager rush of a young family. Among the presents and seated in a child's chair, was a large moth-eaten teddy bear, his arms extended lovingly, his button eyes staring hopefully across the rope which cordoned off the sightseers. As I looked at him, the lights began to dim, the carol-singers were switched off abruptly, and a whistle blew announcing closing time. 'This way out please!' We were shepherded to the door, leaving Sagamore Hill and the teddy bear to loneliness. As we went down the hill to where our car was parked I saw the house was already in darkness. God Rest Ye Merry Teddy Bear, Let Nothing Ye Dismay.

✤   ✤   ✤

And now I have found you again, on an air-strip between Bokhara and Samarcand, and you are still proclaiming your loving-kindness, your message of gentleness. And you are no longer alone.

3

Fragments of a Balkan Journal

The following notes are some made during our two years en poste in the Balkans immediately after the war, from 1946 to 1948. As I saw more of the small details than the whole scene, and a range of local colours rather than purely Red or White interpretations, this is a peep-show on the panorama as it was then, and as I believe much of it remains still, an unchanging backcloth to the shifting scene.

BALKAN FEVER

To love the Balkans is perhaps an acquired taste, but once you have the taste it becomes an obsession. No other scene will do. Capital cities, scenery, comforts, cultures . . . all leave you unmoved, for you are possessed by another love.

This Balkan flavour is hard to define. It is an atmosphere at once subtle and violent, composed of squalor as much as beauty; it does not belong basically to any one country, but is a composite blend of all the Balkan countries: Yugoslavia, Roumania, Albania, Bulgaria, Greece and something of Turkey. It is part Slav, part East. It has no relation to either Hungary or Czecho-slovakia. For me it begins south of Belgrade, though even so flavourless a city produces faint, unexpected whiffs of it, round the flower-market or in the dark, sinister little cafés behind the station. Every time I made the journey to Sofia, those four, five or six-day journeys (for at that moment, the Orient express assumed the pottering character of a local branch line, after Venezia Giulia), I was inert for three-quarters of the way. I sulked through Switzerland; I was restive in Italy. Zagreb passed in a stupor. Such a charming place, a real old Austrian town, everyone said; but what did I want with real old Austrian towns? I was heading for the Balkans, with Bulgaria as the archetype, and the landscape of my heart. I was in a state of torpor until, as the scene both softened and hardened, becoming at once exotic and fierce, I saw again the first place names written in Kyrillic letters. There again were the blue-domed Orthodox churches, the mosques, the great tracts of rich soil ploughed by water buffalo. The solitary figure beside the well, with its primitive contrivance of dipper and long pole balance. The peasants storming the train with their bundles and children and chickens. Someone playing the flute, and everyone singing mournful, haunting chants. It was the Balkans, and I was caught up once more in the old passion.

Around Nish, where the great gorges were edged by a racing pink river, there were unexplained half-a-day halts; the restaurant car had been unhitched and you were lucky to get some bread and salted fish. In the stillness you heard the ox-carts creaking down the mud-track beside the line, and the passengers flung themselves into those timeless political discussions which are the core of Balkan life. With every mile a more Balkanic, and to me more seducing, vista was disclosed. This is the scene I love so deeply, that I carry in my mind's eye always. And each time I returned I was aware of the same trembling excitement, the same beating heart as if I were going to some romantic rendezvous.

Yes and No

Bulgaria is the point on the map where Europe first merges with the East; here the Oriental 'no' prevails. The people nod their heads for 'no', shake them for 'yes'; wildly confusing and amusing to the foreigners. 'They have just come from Europe', the Bulgarians say of visitors, with respect tinged with disapproval, too, in the more perfervid nationalists.

First Glance

There are a few preconceived notions or second-hand opinions about Bulgaria. It was never a 'must' for either the Grand Tour or Cook's. I find it Dionysian and Ruritanian too. The cigar-box-lid landscape of *Arms and the Man* still prevails in spite of the drabness of new standardizations. Beneath it all, the eternal pastoral quality, the unity of man and land. The life of the soil stretching back in an unbroken rhythm, mediaeval, primeval. The roots are pagan. Nothing of the mystical Slav here. Five hundred years of Turkish occupation has left it neither East nor West, but a sort of archetype Balkan middle. Savage Slav qualities mingle with Oriental languors. The landscape echoes this counterpoint. Harsh mountains and exotic prospects, tobacco, vines, roses and rocks.

Counterpoint is everywhere. The gilded domes of the Byzantine churches, the tooth-pick minarets of the mosques. The Rose Mosque blooms out of the snow and slush: Tziganes huddle inside verminous sheepskins flung over their bright, baggy Turkish trousers. Even the language, the root base of later Slav tongues, has many Turkish words grafted on. Names are oddly mixed. Hadji Dimitrov; Sultana Petkanov. Music is at once the sombre religious Slav chant and the voluptuous Oriental *mélopée*, 'a song to be sung in blue mornings', divinely lovely, piercingly sweet, as melting as the frenzied rhythms of the horo are savage.

Last Words

At the cemetery gates, some dramatically minded gardener has contrived two enormous flower-beds spelling out an awesome message. In geraniums, WE TOO WERE ONCE LIKE

YOU. Across the path, in stocks, YOU TOO WILL SOON BE LIKE US.

This is a nice example of the essentially harsh, *masculine* quality of the Bulgarian character, as opposed to the more flowery, Levantine gloss of the cemeteries in Istanbul where elaborate inscriptions on the tombstones make poetic reading. On a child's tomb at Eyüp: 'A flower that had scarcely bloomed, too soon torn from its stem.' On another: 'Here lies one removed to those groves where roses never fade, for they are watered by a mother's tears.' Yet some now strike a positively factual note. On a New Turk's grave I read in French:

Dr. Osman—
nez, gorge, oreilles.

I almost expected to see his consultation hours too!

STREET SCENES

Sofia is small but straggling: you can walk across it in half an hour; but so noisy, cobbles, Red Army lorries, political loudspeakers, argumentative citizens and such, that by comparison, Marseilles is a sleepy market town. Most of the street names have been changed in a gush of tactful enthusiasm. The Boulevard Tzarita Joanna is now named after a Russian statesman.

One should not judge Bulgaria by its capital. There is a Germanic-suburban air in much of Sofia; shoddy art nouveau buildings, with overloaded old trams rattling past fly-blown empty shops. Greasy cobbles, garbage buckets, overstrained, skeletal horses, mangy cats . . . such vistas repel. I do not speak of the great heaps of rubble and bomb damage; I do not notice them. After the war years in London they merely add a homely touch. But Sofia has other aspects. Round the Sobranié, or Parliament, there are painted sugar-ice façades and curlicue balconies, tree-lined boulevards, with a backcloth of distant mountains, all shimmering under a radiant sky, and over all, the great friendly bulk of Vitosha, the mountain which dominates the plain. It is possible to imagine Vitosha without Sofia—but Sofia without its compensating nearness to Vitosha is unthinkable.

Roses Roses all the way

All my life I have heard of Bulgaria's legendary Valley of the Roses; I imagined it to be a sort of botanic gardens, carefully tended parterres, a summer afternoon's stroll. But it is a whole region, twenty miles wide, a hundred miles long, a pink province; at once a tradition and a livelihood: a whole world of its own into which people are born, and where they live and work and die, set a little apart from the rest, and as it were becalmed in fragrance.

It seems there are only a few weeks—in June, when the roses reach their apotheosis. Rose culture demands not only the precise moment of the year, but the exact moment of the day—sunrise. The flowers must be gathered while the dew is still on them, before the heat of the sun has drawn out all their perfume. Today is the first of June. Now is 'the time, and the place': but the loved one . . . ? Romain is not *au fond* interested in tourism. He likes exercise or sport in the fresh air, but shares the general masculine aversion to picnics. Perhaps his French education is responsible for making him feel anything as serious as eating should be undertaken indoors. As to plants, his life has not brought him into contact with them, except in vases on restaurant tables, or as florists' bouquets—*gages d'amour*.

✤   ✤   ✤

On the strict understanding that we shall eat at an inn, no roadside pause with sandwiches, Monsieur Mon Mari agrees to make this expedition. The die was cast when Vladimir (a hireling chauffeur) told us the prettiest peasant girls of all Bulgaria arrive at the Rose Valley to work on the harvest. Vladimir is to take us on a conducted tour. He is of Russian origin, and apt to patronize the Bulgars, as a race—but as women, no man could deny their beauty.

We set out in that hushed, half-darkness before dawn, crossing range after range of the beautiful wild hill country round Karlova, the rose capital. Vladimir explained that a ton of rose petals is required to yield a pound of attar . . . (statistics at such a moment!) We crossed the last pass, and suddenly, were coasting down into a rosy zone, a limbo-land of fragrance. Great wafts of sweetness swept over us, enveloping us, sucking us into a heady ambience. The first level shafts of early sunlight were piercing the haze as we reached the rose planta- tions. As far as the eye could see they stretched ahead in billows of pinkness. At close range, the roses were not such bosomy blooms as I had imagined, but rather austere, single- petalled flowers: yet, the cumulative effect was one of volup- tuousness. The pickers were working up and down the lines of dewy, glittering rose bushes, stripping off the petals and stuffing them into sacks with rhythmic precision. They were singing, the lovely *mélopées* which are a Turkish legacy; the women's heads were bound in lilac or lemon or scarlet silk handker- chiefs, always adorned with a rose; the men, too, wore a bloom stuck jauntily into their high fur kalpaks. I thought of Baudelaire:

> Là, tout n'est qu'ordre et beauté
> Luxe, calme et volupté.

Some of the girls wore stiffly ceremonial dresses of black serge encrusted in gold paillettes which winked in the sunlight. These are traditional garments handed down from one generation to another, and usually worn only on fête days or special occasions. The rose harvest is such. And more, said

Vladimir. The girls go there to catch a beau, the men, to find a wife. As they worked their glances sparked across the foliage—likely lad and comely charmer, pursuit and promise. . . . Love and roses: they are forever linked.

❖   ❖   ❖

We spent the night at Karlova, where distilling factories bring the jam-like sweetness to such a degree that it is almost nauseating. Karlova lies at the end of the Rose Valley and is sheltered from the north by the great scarps of the Rhodope mountains—purple rock, veined with waterfalls, and the setting for much Greek mythology.

'Home of Eurydice', said the innkeeper briefly, displaying that acquaintance with the classics so often found, I have noticed, among the simplest Balkan people.

That night, a messenger came from the Abbess of a nearby convent, inviting us to sup with her. The painted walls of the refectory were bright with childish saints wreathed in garlands —roses, again. The Abbess bowed us to our places with formality. We sat on coarse linen cushions embroidered in stylized scarlet flowers recalling the roses of the world outside. A novice brought us the ceremonial offering, a glass of pure water, and little saucers of translucent rose-leaf jam: this is a Balkan version of the apéritif. The jam induces a fierce thirst, which, it is inferred, can only be slaked by the host's finest wine. Eat, drink and be merry. The convent saw no reason to be otherwise at supper. During the war, they told me, half the rose-crop gave place to baser needs and the Valley of Roses was, in part, the Valley of Potatoes. Even now, we knew conditions were very hard, yet we ate well, among the nuns: great platters of fish from the nearby streams, vegetables simmered in oil, and bowls of yoghourt, all presented with simplicity and style: the style of a people who have never known the vulgarity of commercialism. Vladimir told us the

Abbess had been a great beauty, crossed in love, who found at last consolation in the Church. She had retained all the worldly airs of a hostess. When the bell clanged for prayers and one by one the sisters filed into the dark depths of the chapel, she lingered, telling a peasant's child to lead us to the village square, where the rose-pickers were celebrating their harvest-home with torchlight dances.

'My children, you go with my blessing', she said, and picking red roses off the wall, she pinned them on us with a strangely secular grace.

Under the dense walnut trees, we joined the dancers, who formed a huge circle, hand in hand, spinning faster and faster, while the roses scattered from their heads and lay trampled on the grass.

When at last we returned to the inn, they gave us a nightcap of rose-leaf tea. And there were tight-packed little bouquets of roses on our pillows.

ALL ACCORDING

Life here divides sharply; our kind, the Corps Diplomatique and Allied Control Commission kind, has many privileges. The life lived at present by the bourgeoisie varies from precarious to desperate, with few if any amenities. That lived by the peasants still follows an immemorial rhythm. Dressed in sheepskins, eating bread and onion, toiling from dawn till dusk, their only luxuries tobacco and slivova, a fiery plum brandy. At twilight, the women stop working in the fields, and begin cooking, or spinning their clothes, or household linen. No repose for them by day or night. The men sit in the café, smoking their narghilyé, talking politics, politics, politics, the immemorial Balkan topic. There is another small group, the intelligentsia centred round the theatre and opera, both of which are brilliant. There is no aristocracy as interpreted by the *Almanach de Gotha*.

Last traces of Graustark or Ruritania are found in the Royal Guard, who have stayed on, to adorn the People's junketings. At a government ball given at the Palace last week, they lined the swirling marble stairway, splendidly handsome in a dashing Musée Grévin way, noble chests, richly frogged and padded, and dazzling top-boots, rakish fur shakos, plumed and jewelled.

ODIOUS COMPARISON

Most Bulgarian women are remarkably good-looking. Some are wonderfully beautiful. All of them have an animal vitality. That is, a physical vitality with nothing of the nervous system about it. Repose in them becomes bovinity. Their love of scandal must derive from their oriental blood. Some of the bourgeoises remind me of Cécile in *Les Liaisons Dangereuses:* 'Elle est vraiment délicieuse: cela n'a ni caractère ni principes; jugez combien sa société sera douce et facile.'

FLORA

This country does nothing by halves. Near Sofia there is a lilac forest. A whole forest: another dimension, all colour, into which you can plunge headily. When I spoke of it to Raiina, our Macedonian peasant cook, she began singing some traditional song, *The Lilac-bleeding Star*, strange and poetic as this country I already loved so much.

'Is that an old Bulgarian song?' I asked her, craving for local colour.

'Bulgarian? No indeed!' she spat. 'It comes from *my* Macedonia . . . *Moi Makedonckaya!*' Raiina has a deep sense of unity with her birthplace, and whatever treaties dictate, or ethnographs claim, Macedonia is not Bulgaria, to Raiina. It is something apart—her own.

'And the legend?' I prompt: but Raiina has the cunning of

primitive peoples. She has already discovered that I hang on her words, that I am greedy for the songs and dances and history and customs of Bulgaria; so Raiina is going to dole out her treats, rewarding me with a song, or a story about her uncle, the Bashi-Bazouk (a band of mercenary soldiers, once the terror of the Balkans), when I have been particularly indulgent towards her shortcomings in the kitchen. Fair's fair: she could and often does massacre our meagre rations, but who else would sing of the Lilac-bleeding Star?

FAUNA

Oxen pull the carts everywhere. Trancy white oxen, or the huge horned meek-looking black water-buffaloes. In spring it seems they are liable to turn ugly, and go for anything they see, from a priest to a jeep. These animals were originally imported from Asia. Their ability to survive the Bulgarian climate is remarkable, for when there is heat there is no water, and when there is water there is winter. Meandering along the rice-fields, swaying ponderously, often followed by a moon-faced little calf, they transform the Balkan landscape into something Chinese: one's eye searches for coolies. The fur-capped Bulgarian peasant seems alien, among his own hills. Legends tell that the buffalo will not be hurried. He will work loyally for his master, hour after hour, day after day. But he will not hurry. He knows he is a heavy, clumsy creature. He does not wish to stampede along, bruising the good earth he loves.

ORTHODOX AND UNORTHODOX DEVOTIONS

The Alexander Nevski Cathedral boasts a magnificent bass singer. He rolls out huge earthy belly notes which resound through the Byzantine domes, rising and falling again, lost in the shimmer of candlelight that glows up from the floor, where candles are ranged in memory of the dead. The Orthodox service is a free, spontaneous affair: it has none of that dank low-church rigidity, nor yet the tawdry theatricality of the Papists. People stroll in and out with bundles, children; soldiers stamp their snowy boots, dump their rifles; there are Russian soldiers too. Since there are no seats, the whole church is a shifting mass of dark figures, silhouetted against the candles. They kiss the ikons, or prostrate themselves before the iconostas. There are peasants who have tethered their oxen at the door, seedy old men who stand, as if transfixed by time, and always, in the darkest corners, curious little groups of two or three, strange-looking individuals, unshaven, coat collars turned up, who seem to be met there on some sinister purpose; whose muttering always ceases as you approach. The Tziganes insinuate themselves here, too, and whine softly as they go from person to person, their slyly seducing faces supplicating, their dirt-caked palms turned up expectantly. And Bortniansky's music is everywhere.

PRE-GIOTTO

In the tiny church at Boyjana, hidden among the plumed foliage of Vitosha's lower slopes, the eleventh-century frescoes are strong proof of that simplicity, of bucolic matter-of-factness—nothing mystical here—with which the Bulgarians overcame the rigid conventions of Byzantine art. And this at a time when Giotto was yet to be born, and the stylized traditions of the ikon were accepted from Constantinople to Novgorod. Yet here, in this remote village, we see the breaking of that tradition, and a bold move towards realism. The faces are human, warm, natural faces, and very Slav, with their play of emotion. Naturalistic details abound. The Last Supper is presented in such a manner that it becomes an historic document, a testimony of daily life. We see the table and linen and dishes of that moment. And how unchanging the scene, then and now: everyone is eating onions!

PINK AND WHITE

Among the most primitive peasants of the mountain villages, you will sometimes see a bizarre *maquillage* still worn by the young girls. This is the red and white of the painted doll: they still use a deadly sort of white pigment which blanches the skin for a while, and ends by poisoning them.

These daubed Balkan faces, so roundly rouged, probably aim at an effect of dazzling freshness, the kind to which Gogol so often refers in *Dead Souls*. 'She was as fresh as blood and milk', he says, with relish: no effete comparison to roses here; it is more in the tradition of the bold scarlet circles painted on the cheeks of high-bred Mongolian beauties. But the Bulgarian *maquillage* is only a passing trick to catch a boy. As soon as she is married, which is often at fourteen or thereabouts, the bride's paint is gone for good. And soon after, her beauty goes too. The peasants age rapidly, becoming wrinkled slaves to their men, who are still treated like pashas, riding ahead on the donkey, while the women drag along behind, bent double under their burdens. Bulgaria retains many oriental customs. It used to be the custom, and still is in some parts, for the woman to stand at a respectful distance from the table while her lord and master eats.

MADAME TIGGY WINKLI

The last few days have been particularly lowering; international tensions at breaking point all round. The Minister being in Switzerland on sick leave, Romain is Chargé d'Affaires. His long ikon-face is thunderous. Waiting for a stream of government instructions to be decoded is nerve-racking to all of us. Draga V. has been given an exit visa by the Russians, but her relatives don't seem relieved. They've been besieging us all day, sobbing and wailing, asking if she can travel with our courier. They seem to be a morbid lot, convinced Draga's breasts will be sliced off at the Yugoslavian frontier. Romain says it is a classic Balkan gesture.

It has snowed for forty-eight hours. Vitosha is blotted out. Our newspapers are two weeks old. There is no opera this week, even if we could get through the snow-drifts. Romain returns home more ikon-faced than ever. Nothing distracts him. Last night, I suddenly remembered how he used to enjoy the Beatrix Potter books when he was learning English. He still refers to *The Flopsie Bunnies* as *La Famille Flopsaut*. I rang the British Legation.

'Mary, have you by any chance got *Mrs. Tiggy Winkle?* Romain would *so* enjoy her just now.'

'Yes, as a matter of fact I think we have. If the snow's not too thick I'll send her round at once.'

A distant but distinct click on the telephone. Tapped again. I wondered what the circuitous minds of the listeners would make of Mrs. Tiggy Winkle. Some dangerously seductive Mata-Hari character no doubt. I imagined the scene at the Deuxième Bureau. 'Teegee Weenkli? Who is she? Find out at once! Put a guard round the place . . . mark who comes and goes. Madame Teegee Weenkli . . . ? Hold her for interrogation . . . And you say his *own wife* was asking for her? Those French!'

WAYS AND MEANS

The housing shortage is acute. Our present apartment is hideously furnished, and in an inaccessible quarter. But one of the kavas at the Legation has told us that they are expecting a big purge, soon, in which case, there will be better accommodation to be had for the asking.

'Do you think he *realized* what he was saying?'
'Mm . . . This is the Balkans.'

SACRED AND PROFANE

Rila Monastery is said to be the most holy place in all
Bulgaria. But to me it has an oddly secular, almost frivolous
air. Its architecture is pastry-cooks' delight, striped pink and
white and yellow like a layer cake. Picnic parties merge with
pilgrims: in their snugly furnished cells the monks entertain
their friends. The sumptuously gilded, opera-house en-
crustations in the church make it seem less religious than the
little souvenir shop in the courtyard, full of cheap ikons and
holy oleographs.

The first time I went to Rila, we arrived around mid-day,
after a four hours' drive from Sofia, by Dupnitza, up and up,
always mounting into the high ravine country of the Rila
mountains. We drove into the courtyard at full tilt. It was a
Sunday. There were several charabancs full of devout pilgrims,
a Red Army sightseeing bus, and a lorry-load full of Coldstream
Guards, part of the Allied Control Commission personnel.
We went first to pay our official visit to the Igumen, or Abbot,
who received us most kindly. He spoke beautiful French, and
had been a distinguished lawyer. We sat on divans covered in
fine rugs, and were given the traditional *sladko* of welcome,
spoonfuls of honey, and little blue glasses of a fierce yet mellow
liqueur they make at the monastery.

Back in the courtyard once more, we were flies, caught in
the guide's web. Struggling desperately to free ourselves we
were spun from museum to chapel, from cloister to bell-tower.
We even walked into his parlour, a pretty little cell with a
painted and carved pink and blue ceiling. We visited several
of these cells. Anything less monastic, less mortifying, could
not be imagined. Some had electric bells, others had yale locks.
Brother Timofi showed us his with beaming pride. There was
a white stone stove, an iron bedstead decorated with painted
panels representing the Bay of Naples at the head and the
Château of Chillon at the foot, a number of bright, gros-point

cushions on the bed and a horribly embroidered and fringed table cloth. Plants trailed over the deep window-sills, and there were quantities of family photographs and football team groups, which proved on closer inspection to be monks arranged in the same pyramid form, arms crossed and button eyes glassily fixed. The captain, or in this case, the Igumen, was in the centre holding an ikon in place of the football usually associated with such groups.

Did I say Rila was frivolous? It is positively operetta. There was a constant coming and going across the cobbles: a white-capped cook bargained with a pedlar: carpenters hammered and sang. A mechanically minded pilgrim tinkered with his motor bicycle. With raucous laughter, two American sergeants bought a wooden backscratcher from the souvenir-stall. There was all the movement of a market-town inn.

The famous frescoes round the church are riotously gay, painted with a child's paint-box. Fork-tailed devils are heartily enjoying the seven deadly sins. Biblical scenes painted with jolly gusto, such blue, blue skies, such pink, pink temples, such smiling, red-faced lions, such Turkish-trousered saints, such rakish haloes . . . Rila is a holy land in terms of Images d'Épinal.

After lunch we were overcome, and profited by the Igumen's hospitable offer of the one-time Royal Suite, for a siesta. Returning refreshed to the touristic assault, we encountered some of the Coldstream Guards, who, along with their young ladies (mostly luscious local brunettes) had been offered similar hospitality by resident pilgrims. They were describing it as a bit of all right.

At four o'clock exactly, we heard the famous wooden clapper-board call to prayer sounding down the striped arcades. When the Turks forbade church bells, the monks made do with a curious system of sounding-board or *klepalo*, still in use. A brisk, booted monk came striding towards us, his black robes flapping, his long board, like a narrow, loose paling, which he struck with a wooden mallet; the sound changed according to where he hit it. He flapped his way twice round the courtyard, marked time for some amateur photographers and then led the way into the church, followed by the Red Army, the Coldstream Guards and ourselves. The service seemed a casual affair: tourists and pilgrims went in and out, noisily. There was no singing: the brothers intoned the old Slav chants, their rich, gravy voices echoing impressively. The reek of incense wafted over the garlic-blasting peasants, a counterpoint of odours, sacred and profane.

Against the gilding of the iconostas, there was a crudely painted coffin, with chintzy roses on a scarlet ground, containing the sarcophagus of St. John of Rila. The opening of this coffin is the high spot of the afternoon service. I hung around. Presently the painted lid was raised. Layers of gauze and silk were parted to reveal a peep of mummified flesh, sticky brownish holy of holies. The true believers pressed forward to kiss it in ecstasies of devotion. Both the Coldstream Guards and the Red Army stood firm.

You can book a cell at Rila and stay there as long as you please, surrounded by other pilgrims, cooking in the little anterooms attached to the cells, or in the enormous mediaeval dining-hall of the monastery, or at the new restaurant that has been built beside the ravine; you can attend the services, or walk in the mountains. Such a sojourn can scarcely be called a retreat in the religious sense, however Romain and I think we might enjoy staying here. The rushing torrent cascades beneath the deep-embrasured windows. All around are the peaks of the mountains, sombre and remote. But however pearly-pure the cells appear, I'm told bugs are inevitable. The state of most pilgrims makes it a lost battle. As to the sanitation at Rila—there is nothing frivolous about that. A tower, hanging over a ravine, and a hole in the floor over the steepest drop. Guides—bugs—sanitation. Perhaps these are Rila's special means of mortifying the flesh.

Bulgaria

THE HORO

Everyone dances the *horo*. The soldiers, whiling away an hour on the barrack square; the government officials and their wives at the big political functions; the villagers on Sunday evenings; and the foreigners, more rapturously than skilfully. A great ring-o'-roses, stamping criss-cross steps, wilder and wilder; pursuit and retreat, immemorial coquetry. The Tziganes have their own specially vicious way of stamping, and they roll their bellies in a sort of *danse du ventre*, called here the *Kadunjiebek*. *Horo* music heard from afar produces a curious *frisson*, a sort of sinister, galvanic attraction.

At the Russian Embassy the little white and gold ballroom was very Petersburg, 1820. I expected to see Tatiana and Onegin come dashing down the parquet in a polonaise. Large wash-basin-sized bowls of caviar were loaded along the buffet. Vodka flowed. Everyone began to dance the *horo*, medals bounced, buttons burst. In the crimson and gold velvet ante-chamber the Exarkh and the high clergy sat in a little black clot, like beetles in jam.

LITTLE VISITORS

I went out to the airfield to help welcome two planeloads of French children who were invited to spend a month's holiday in the mountains as guests of the Bulgarian children. It was searingly hot on the tarmac. A number of Russian machines were lined up being refuelled, and some Russian officers and their families came out of the main building to watch the arrival. Every few minutes lorry-loads of spanking fine Bulgarian children arrived, singing, waving branches of evergreen, and carrying clumsily but lovingly lettered banners saying, WELCOME TO OUR LITTLE FRENCH COMRADES.

It was all rather moving. The woman whose idea it had been is a dynamic figure, known as *La Pasionaria* of the Balkans.

43

Her life has been one of violent drama, in the course of which she has been four times condemned to death. Still, she was now quite overcome, and melted into tears. So did the Soviet mechanics; and the swarthy ground crews sobbed too, as the planes circled the field. The children were becoming over-excited, beginning their welcome addresses too soon, or having to be rushed off to the lavatory at top speed. The Soviet soldiers hustled them back, all nicely buttoned, well before the planes taxied in.

As the planes came to a standstill, there was a glimpse of pale sickly faces and sticky paws pasted on the windows. The Bulgarian children surged forward, and the reception committee was engulfed in the Lilliputian wave. The French children, looking dreadfully thin and wan (they were picked from very poor families and slum districts which suffered particularly during the Nazi occupation) now came tumbling out banging their heads and barking their shins. The smallest Bulgarian boy, who was entirely extinguished by a mammoth bouquet of gladioli then piped up with an address of welcome in florid French. It was infinitely touching: an ideal of friendship put into practice. Well might the Bulgarian Committee glow with pride, well might there be sobbing and rejoicing.

✤   ✤   ✤

Five weeks later the children returned from their camp at Kostenetz, and on the eve of their return flight there was a big farewell party at our Legation. They filed in, rosy, and bulging out of their new clothes—the Bulgarians had re-equipped them splendidly. 'They weigh five kilos more than when they arrived, and they all speak Bulgarian,' said their governess. They remained crimson and tongue-tied with us however. We led them to the buffet where a rich array of pastries was displayed. They stood in solid formation, like some massed choir, one behind the other five deep, stoking rhythmically. One small boy was wearing a very fine embroidered peasant handkerchief tucked in the breast pocket of his sailor suit. I admired it and in so doing, twitched it out, so that several fag-ends were dislodged, and rolled under the table. It was a terrible moment; we avoided each other's eyes and spoke of other things. At last they had eaten enough, and the treacly dregs had been drained. We packed them into their charabancs.

'Yes, indeed, it is most gratifying,' said an elderly gentleman with white moustachios, who had been closely concerned with the whole scheme. 'The boys are fine specimens now, and the girls—' he cast a luxuriously lingering glance over the nubile forms bursting so promisingly out of the charabanc windows— 'the little girls have all become young ladies,' he said, and sighed, and went home.

OFF WITH THE RAGGLE-TAGGLE GYPSIES O!

Moving house is always a maddening moment, but something of the exasperation seems to be taken out, here, because Raiina obtained the services of a celebrated pair of Tziganes. In Bulgaria the Tziganes are held to be master-movers. They bring science to their art, balance grand pianos on the nape of their necks in the precise spot calculated to bear the strain. Suddenly galvanized they swing immense weights about and juggle with packing-cases. Round the markets the streets are always full of Tziganes wearing peaked caps, and hung with stout ropes, lounging around, waiting to pick up some bit of porterage.

Apart from the fact they arrived three hours late, drank most of my remaining French Cognac, and asked the equivalent of a Bulgarian Cabinet Minister's salary, the Tziganes were excellent. I found their antics, their padding bare feet and chatter an exotic diversion. But comparing them to the British removal-man, there were certain basic differences. They were quicker—once they began—and there was less of that straining immobility, that 'To you! To you, Ernie'—or 'Take it your end, Bert!' that accompanies a deadlock on the stairs at home. But they were not good organizers and had no sense of time (or fortunately, of overtime). By nightfall they had succeeded in piling all our belongings into the van, which they then placed in a side street. While one settled down among the crates, to sleep there and guard it, he said, till morning, the other unharnessed the horse and made off towards the *mahalla*. My shrieks did not turn him.

'He has a young and beautiful wife,' said the van-watcher. He flashed his splendid teeth and made an unmistakably ribald gesture. Only after a lot of silver had crossed his palm would he consent to extract our bed and set this up in our bare new lodging. Even so, there were no pillows, and only one blanket.

'Such springs!' said the Gypsy, prodding with a dusty finger, 'who would want to sleep?' He made another of those jolly, international gestures called obscene and left us to reflect on the advantages of employing regular removers. I thought longingly of Harrods' white-aproned teams, but Romain, having spent a number of years fleeing across frontiers with nothing, and living afterwards in hotels, or barracks, does not share my preoccupations with the classic comforts of the home.

WINTER PIECE

Each morning, from my new window I see the manège as a woodcut. The unbroken square of white snow is ringed by the barracks, their eaves festooned with five-foot icicles. A bugle blows thinly in the knife-cold air: out comes the cavalry. A ring of horsemen begin to prance round the square, black, very black against the snow. Round and round they go, rocking-horse cavalry, the horses snorting and cavorting,

Dobbin-like. The breath steams out of their nostrils in grey puffs. Overhead the rooks circle, cawing. It is a world of wood-cut values, black on white. Another bugle sounds. The cavaliers trot off towards the stables. The horses sidle and shy at the ice puddles by the fountain. It is breakfast time. Raiina lights the samovar and says the soldiers will be eating bread and paprika, and drinking rose-leaf tea. They must be the only troops to start their day on such an exotic brew.

SENSE OF HUMOUR

Humour is of the broad order, here (though the people themselves are of a rather dour nature).

But one finds it hard to believe there is no irony in their habit of employing likely and unlikely adjectives for shop-keepers' names. This choice of adjectives is an endless entertainment to us, and Romain and I collect and swap them daily. Mr. Bones the Butcher may be 'Tender' Bones, or he may just as easily be 'Fragrant', 'Merry' or 'Gracious'. The barber's shop is labelled 'Eternal Beauty' Stoyanov. The funeral undertakers are perhaps the best examples of this *jeu:* 'Last Care' Petkanov, 'Dust' Zdravkov, or my favourite, Bezoumna Skroub, 'Frenzied Mourning' Ivanov.

ONOMATOPOEIA

Bulgarian place-names are particularly expressive. They have an almost onomatopoeic felicity. Pamporovo is light, fluffy with snow, like its mountains. Ichtiman is mean, ingrown. Dragalevtzi is a Slav fairy-tale name, direct from the Skazki, or legends. So is Malevitza, which might be the name of an enchanted princess. Sredna Gora—the name is as dramatic as the mountain range which is steeped in the blood of revolt. But Karlovo is all warmth and softness, to match the little pink town among the walnut trees in the Rose Valley. Bachkovo is dark-sounding, noble, as befits the monastery built by two Georgian princes in the eleventh century and which commands a ravine of the Black Balkans. Madara is as languorous and oriental in appearance as its sound. Messemvria seems to hum and shimmer in a heat haze with its Black Sea coast-line. Pernik is all harsh clangour, like its mines. Loveliest of all, to me, the Rhodope and the Pachmakli; proud names that breathe all the poetic beauty and wildness of their region.

THE MILKY WAY

The incredible longevity of the Bulgarians is attributed to their staple diet of yoghourt, or *kisselomlieko* to give it the correct Slav name. However, until a few years back there were no birth certificates, so that no reliable reckoning could be made. After seventy pride works in the reverse, I've noticed, and there is more interest in claiming to be a hundred and seven. One alleged centenarian, a retired general, has just remarried for the fifth time. His bride is in her seventies.

'*Mariage blanc,* my dear sir,' the old gentleman assures all those who congratulate him. But the bride seems offended by this assertion.

ETHNOLOGICAL TIT-BITS

Bulgaria contains a great number of strange sects and tribes. Least known, the Karakachans, who live on the high plateaux and are both wild and disagreeable. In this community the women, who are thickly veiled, do all the work, building huts, chopping wood, hunting for game.... The men consent to breed, but no more. When I recounted this at a dinner party, the assembled gentlemen, particularly the Americans, looked sadly envious.

En Route

At a station near Nish the darkness was profound. A few oil lamps were set on the ground beside a group of men surrounded by soldiers. The sickly flicker lit up pale, tired faces and the soldiers' accoutrements. Suddenly, they began singing, a wild, proud and mournful chant. Everyone listened, stilled by the majesty of the song. Along the corridor of the *wagon-lits* the international chit-chat died away. Such singing, such a quality of emotion is not heard often. I flung myself down on to the platform and approached the group. They had stopped as abruptly as they had begun and I wanted to ask them to sing once more. As I reached them, a soldier picked up a lantern. The light glinted on the chains that shackled the men, one to another. What they had done, where they were going, I shall never know: but I shall always remember how they sang.

Blood Sacrifice

It is said that every July the Black Sea claims a victim. This year has been no exception. A small child was drowned before its parents' eyes, in a few feet of water. When the body was recovered, the whole *plage* set up a cry that was terrifying to hear. It was the abandoned grief of the Orient; tearing at their hair and faces, wailing and gnashing, and striking an even more terrible note, coming from the play-suited, sun-bathing, Westernized crowds on the sands.

Two Ceremonies

Atanass is a small Tzigane who begs outside the Alexander Nevski Cathedral. Sometimes he is alone, sometimes with his mother, who has been a great beauty. Both of them are tattooed with the crescent and star of Islam on their foreheads, barely discernible through the layers of dirt. They are old friends of Raiina, who knew them when she worked in the tobacco factory at Plovdiv and they were lolling in the sun-baked mud of Mahallah, a violently picturesque Gypsy quarter just outside the town. Atanass's mother was persuaded (by Nedi, a friend from whom all kindness flows) to come and show the sewing-woman how to cut *chalvaari*, which are the complicated, gracefully draped trousers most Tzigane women wear. I had followed a number of Tziganes about, trying to see how they were made but without success, for they are far from being the simple, bunched or twisted garments they appear.

Atanass's mother thoughtfully brought along an old pair belonging to her family for me to try on and I had great difficulty in avoiding such a dress rehearsal. However, it all went off well. Mme. Violetta, as the local sewing-woman prefers to be called, cut the *toile*, and Atanass's mother crouched on her haunches, directing operations and drinking Cointreau, which Raiina said was all she fancied that morning. I crossed her palm and we parted the best of friends.

A few days later she invited me to a Gypsy wedding. There is a very large Gypsy population in Bulgaria. Like the Jews and other minorities they have so far lived in freedom, having their own language, customs and schools. Most of the big towns have a Gypsy quarter. At Kustendil they live in caves in the mountain gorges of the Blue Rocks. At Madara their little coloured shacks are built all over the cliff-face. They are everywhere. Nomadic or static they live much the same way. Their encampments of painted carts (they do not have caravans) and black tents are all along the roads. They sprawl, splendidly indolent, on the piles of sheepskins which, as Listz said in his book on Gypsy music, are their only furniture.

The wedding was to be held in the Gypsy quarter, in the straggling western outskirts of Sofia, beyond the Jewish quarter. Here, the mud and dust streets trail off into shacks, refuse heaps, tin cans, dead cats. The city stops abruptly, as if at some invisible barrier. Suddenly, there are no more houses, and you are in the great plain of Sofia, ringed all round with the crumpled, pie-crust edge of mountains. 'Ulitza Tartarli 27' said the screw of paper which was the invitation. The street of the Tartars, of the Tziganes. It was easy to find, for there was a sound of music and it was hung with paper flowers and ribbons. It was a long, wide unpaved street lined with little shacks, fenced with broken-down palings, over which rather seedy vines trailed. Tziganes do not have green fingers. The entire population seemed to live outside, cooking on braziers, or lolling on rags, or broken iron bedsteads, set under the stumpy acacia trees. I thought how terribly squalid such a scene must look in the rain; but the long, certain, golden summer suns of Sofia gild and soften everything.

They were dancing a *horo* outside No. 27, spinning round, shrieking, their bare blackened feet kicking up clouds of dust. They all crowded round, very friendly, almost menacing in their advances. The children lifted my skirt and peeped beneath. The women put their arms round me and fingered my hair. It seems that, as the guest of Atanass's mother, I was warmly welcome. The men, slouching in the doorways half-naked, pulled their caps down over their eyes and leered amiably. The babies, who were completely naked except for a string of blue amulet beads, swarmed round chattering and grimacing; they looked scabrous. Little girls of twelve or thereabouts were gaudily painted, and wore a flower behind one ear. They had all the calculated coquetry of the prostitute. These were the degenerate mongrel Tziganes, corrupted by city life, with none of the pride and tradition of the pure breed: but with the same impelling fascination.

Atanass's mother now appeared, in great confusion at having been absent when I arrived. She launched into a flood of explanation which I did not follow and led me towards one of the houses, pursued by the crowd. Tzigane women walk magnificently. They carry their babies on their shoulder like little princes. But it is always startling to see what appears to be an old, wrinkled creature, a toothless hag, sometimes, as the mother of a tiny baby. At thirty-five, Gypsy women look sixty. The really old crones become ageless mummies, rag-bags, smoking incessantly, pickled in nicotine. Inside the hut, I was presented to a stoutish middle-aged Tzigane wearing a well-preserved top-hat, which, being alien to the Balkans, he had no doubt inherited from the valet of some visiting diplomat. Atanass's mother said he was the king of the Gypsies and I daresay he was. Alas! he said, the wedding was postponed till next week. Meanwhile, there was to be another celebration, a big fête, that night. He hoped I would stay.

'What ceremony?' I asked.

'A circumcision', he explained, with graphic gestures.

This is always a solemn occasion in Mohammedan circles. Already the street was filling up from all around: the band, reinforced by a drum, was going all out. I was pushed into the blue-washed yard, where the victim was led up and introduced. He was a pale ox-eyed boy of about ten years old, sickly with pride and a sense of his destiny. He wore a patent leather peaked cap decorated with ferns and silver beads. His parents now led me to the room prepared for the ceremony. Impelled by ghoulish curiosity, I followed. As a rule, Tzigane huts are completely bare except for a pile of bedding, the stove, and a shelf of tins and crockery. But this room was filled with chairs, and had a bedstead, transformed into a four-poster, with lace curtains. There were gaudy rugs on the wall, and a large, coloured shampoo-show-card, showing a lush couple in full evening dress, embracing passionately beneath a tropic moon. Several electric-light bulbs hung from the ceiling: they were decorated with frills of coloured paper, and dangling below, in the manner of Christmas-tree decorations, were a number of life-like representations of a penis covered in silver paper, a chocolate-box touch, I thought.

The room was suffocatingly hot. The dedicated child stood proudly beside me, smoking a presentation cigarette (gold-tipped), in a self-conscious way. More and more Tziganes pressed in. I imagined I could feel the fleas leaping across to me, as virgin ground. I was writhing with discomfort, when the violent rhythm of drum and pipe brought everyone out into the street. Another band, all Turkish traditional instruments, was escorting a large sheep, carried pick-a-back by a gruesome-looking idiot, who pranced along, apparently unaware of the sheep's weight. I'm not sure if the animal was to be a sacrifice or eaten next day, but in any case, I fear its days were numbered. At the moment, however, it seemed quite comfortable; they are accustomed to being carried in this way: I have often seen the shepherds wearing a huge live shaggy sheep over their shoulders, rather in the manner of those silver fox ties once the height of fashion. The band was decorated with green branches and now broke into a peculiar version of some old American dance tune and which sounded oddly on the *gusla* and *kaval*; I thought I recognized *Mean To Me*. Nedi says they dote on ' Jazz-ki'.

Everyone began to dance. Tziganes never dance in couples as we do: men dance with men, women with women. Now the rhythm changed and they formed a chain. They were off, wildly stamping into their own kind of *horo*. Nursing mothers leapt along with tiny babies still clutching their bare breasts. The older ones, just able to sit up, though with lolling heads, were spun round and round like Dervishes. One by one the dancers collapsed on to the sagging bedsteads. Some flung themselves down beside the old crones who were cooking, or went back to their former occupation of delousing a neighbour's head. I was offered a delicious snack of some sort of pimento and bean stew. But afterwards, I had to tear myself away reluctantly. The ceremony proper showed no signs of beginning and I remembered guiltily that I was supposed to be at an inter-Legation all-ladies tea-party, quite a different kind of gathering. As I drove back towards the more refined quarters of the town and the wail of the *kaval* was drowned by the clang of the trams, the driver told me how such ceremonies usually end with the victim being conducted through the streets in glory to the public baths to be ritualistically cleansed. This is equalled by the traditional wedding ceremonies of the Bulgarian peasants who wait outside the bridegroom's house when he takes his bride home. And if, as it is hoped, she is proved a virgin, a special symbolic red-tinged *rakia* is drunk in her honour.

PLAIN SPEAKING

I don't dislike Chamkouria—I detest it. It is the only place in all Bulgaria which I hate. The dank pine forests close round the chilly chalets, shutting out the sun. To me, it is imitation Switzerland, nothing Bulgarian. All Sofia, the so-called 'hij-lif' set, that is, used to gather at Chamkouria till it was like a sort of social concentration camp. In winter, skiing; in summer, fishing. Horribly adjacent, the chalets impinge on one another. Everybody is aware of everybody else's slightest movement. Gossip throbs through the glades like some African tom-tom. Yet it continues to attract both Sofiotes and visitors; week-end after week-end they desert the benign and open villages round the slopes of Vitosha in favour of these sinister chalets, as artificial, as menacing as the witches' gingerbread house of Hansel and Gretel.

SHIPKA

Shipka Monastery starts out from the spinach-green firs as you descend the pass of the same name. It is a cleft in two mountains, scene of the decisive victory of 1877. It was here that the Russians took their stand beside the Bulgarians, who battled to overthrow the Turkish yoke. The pass seems awkwardly chosen as a battlefield. Dragging the guns up and the wounded down must have been an appalling labour. It was a holocaust. For three days and nights six thousand Bulgarians held the pass against forty thousand Turks. When the Cossack reinforcements arrived there was no more ammunition left, and the Bulgarians were hurling down the corpses of their comrades on to the advancing Turks. There is a celebrated canvas by Verestchaguin, the Russian painter who was particularly inspired by the horrors of warfare: strewn battle-fields in the snow, towers of skulls, or scenes of carnage in the Russians' Central Asian campaigns. He left several paintings of the Russo-Turkish war; 'All is Quiet on the Shipka Pass', the words of a much-cited dispatch (which was later to be echoed by *All Quiet on the Western Front*), depicts a Russian sentry, frozen to death, guarding the pass with its frozen corpses.

Shipka Monastery looks like some celestial toy set down among the hills. The golden fish-scale cupolas glitter in the sun, flashing pink and crimson and gold. It was begun soon after the victory, in celebration; but it was only completed a few years ago. Now it serves as a sort of hospital-almshouse for a few incapacitated Russian soldiers of the 1914–18 war, who, somehow, found themselves marooned in the Balkans. Last summer the Soviets put up another stone monolith on the hills above the monastery, to commemorate the new generation of Russian soldiers who fell in Bulgaria. The church is dis-illusioning, at close quarters: garish, art-nouveau in type, lined with plaques listing the fallen Russian regiments. Bulgarians and Russians lie side by side with nameless Turks in their communal graves. Once again, all is quiet on the Shipka Pass.

PURSUIT OF BEAUTY

At the hairdresser's I plough on with my Bulgarian, while someone pours kettles of too hot or too cold water over

55

me. Radka, the pretty proprietor pins my set, while her old peasant mother crouches by the big stove—as a mark of special esteem I am always given the cubicle with the stove—and Radka's handsome husband Mitko holds the pins and tells me how he used to play Prince Danilo in *The Merry Widow* in Macedonia. And then, while I'm under the dryer, Radka has a rest and sits on Mitko's knee swinging her Russian booted legs: the children are brought in for me to admire and we discuss Radka's chances of winning a prize, if she can get to Paris for the next International Coiffeur Contest, and we drink to it in slivova.

STUDY IN RED

If one can limit one's mind's-eye view of a country to any one colour (without any political implication, of course), I suppose red, a glowing pinkish red would be the predominant Bulgarian colour. France has an all-over pearly-grey hue which is more of a light, an ambience, than a colour. England is green—where it isn't a sooty drab. In old Slav, red has always been synonymous with beauty. In Russia, 'Krassivie', beautiful, stems from 'Krassnie', red—or the other way about. 'Krassa' is beauty. In Moscow, the 'Red' Square also means the 'Beautiful'. The Skazki are full of young princes who wear blood-red robes: the peasant boy who wins the princess always wears a red *roubashka*. The walls of the old churches and monasteries are often painted a deep crimson. Rastrelli's original design for the Winter Palace was a burning orange, but this was changed to a dark red; either colour must have glowed out from the snow or rains of St. Petersburg. Various religious sects carried a red handkerchief as symbol of their martyrdom.

There are many examples, such as the Bulgarian custom of exchanging and wearing red and white tokens, or *porte bonheur* —Martenitza—on the first of March, which again show the superstitious regard the Slav peoples feel for red. The banners and badges of the Red Army continue the tradition. And the Bulgarian country has a pervading red note. The earth varies from a bright brick to purple-red. The walls of the peasant houses are pink-washed; blue, too, it must be admitted: but with their overhanging red-tiled roofs, their wide balconies festooned with blazing red pimentos hung out to dry, with the tumble of roses everywhere, the broad red cummerbund every peasant man wears, and the great tracts of forest, burnished to scarlet by the long, fierce autumn suns, then Bulgaria seems to vibrate in a reddish glow.

ECCLESIASTICAL SHORTCOMINGS

The British Legation is in a ferment, for His Grace the Bishop of Gibraltar's visit is scheduled for next week. His diocese stretches exotically from Gibraltar to Baku, with Bulgaria en route. The Anglo-Saxon colony, including the Americans, have decided on a mass christening of those children as yet unconsecrated. Since there is no suitable church, the service is to be held in the drawing-room of the Legation. But H.M.s' Office of Works furnishings (near-Hepplewhite dining-room, and 'safe' chintzes in the drawing-room) does not include a font. The Press Attaché has been scouring the countryside for some suitable receptacle: so far, he has been unsuccessful, and the colony are faced with the alternative of a soup-tureen or a bird-bath.

CIRCUS IN THE SNOW

When winter clamps down, in December, Romain goes for an early-morning work-out in a nearby gymnasium. It is also the winter quarters of a circus, then training for the spring season. This is very distracting. Buxom charmers in tights ogle him, hanging upside down by their teeth. Wire-walkers flirt over the top of Japanese parasols. They are coached by a seedy old man, wildly moustached, wearing a fur cap and bedroom slippers, Bai Pentcho, the king of Bulgarian circus, and seventy years in the ring. He used to pinch the young ladies, as they swarmed round, and has offered to coach my husband in a trapeze act. When this offer was declined, he presented him with his memoirs, flowerily inscribed, from one author to another. This proved to be a Don Juan travelogue, very racy reading.

Perhaps the most powerful distraction is Fintcho, a fox-terrier passionately anxious to perform on all occasions, for ever teetering around on his hind legs, waltzing, spinning, tumbling, in ecstasies of creative abandon. Winter is dull for him, his owner says; he frets; he misses his public. He spends much time curled in the vast lap of Bai Pentcho's fourth wife, now tight-darner for the show, a sad come-down, for she had been the most sensational snake-charmer of the Near East.

Postcript: Soon after leaving Bulgaria I read in the papers that the leaders of the Sofia circus had gone to Moscow for a refresher course. They had been taxed with 'formalism, and lack of constructive purpose'. It was hoped that their visit would bring them into line with 'Socialist Realist Art'. I wonder how this affected Fintcho?

OATEN STOP

A vast expanse of sky and earth. An endless horizon of far distances. Sheep moving slowly, their bells sounding across the hills. Shepherds stand like graven figures, immobile, beneath their long striped cloaks. Sometimes there is the thin plaintive note of a flute or reed pipe, reaching back into the pastoral childhood of the world. Bulgaria is perhaps the last truly pastoral country of Europe: it is this deep sense of unity with the earth, this Theocritan quality which I remember most now I am far, far away.

4

Raiina—a Balkan Cook

Raiina was the first Bulgarian I knew well, and she has remained, for me, the personification of all I love best in the Balkans. I dreaded my last farewells and I miss her still. I shall always remember her, as I shall always remember Bulgaria.

She was my cook, a Macedonian peasant, dark, violent, obstinate, loving and loyal. She had a strangely ape-like intelligence and appearance, the same pushed-in monkey-mug, the same beautiful, golden, pathetic eyes. She could be darting-quick and full of primitive cunning. And she could be dull and lethargic, particularly when not in agreement with me, dragging about the kitchen slow as a deep-sea diver. Raiina instantly assumed that we should be able to converse together in a pigeon-blend of Russian and Bulgarian; and though, when I arrived I had small Russian and no Bulgarian, it worked out well. The desperate necessities of one kitchen crisis after another, combined with the vivid daily drama of Raiina's home-life was a forcing-house for me. In a few months we were able to discuss anything, from Balkan divorce laws to techniques for dealing with the inevitable bugs.

In Sofia even D.D.T. was useless, for this determined pest lurked in the flat below and merely bided its time before returning to the attack. And as the flat below contained four separate families, all packed in, to conform with new housing regulations, but who were indifferent to such minor trials, I came to accept them, too, and contented myself with burning them on sight. Raiina was wonderfully skilful at slaying them with a lighted match, while yet leaving their terrain, whether furniture, or bedding, unsinged. I never acquired the technique of some Balkan gentlemen who used to nip them to death between their curiously long finger-nails.

Raiina's family, who played a large part in our lives, were introduced to me almost before I was unpacked. They were always with us, whether in Sofia, or on the Black Sea. Tomislav, her drunken, dissolute husband, a house-painter by fits and starts, was seldom seen—he lurked in the background, a sinister figure from whom all evil flowed. But the children, Minka, Lili, Radka and Borislav—a savage, gargantuan baby whom Raiina was nursing, to the detriment of our household routine, and the astonishment of neatly gloved Corps Diplomatique callers, when she opened the door with the monster brat clinging limpet-like to her bare breast, were at once a living, and very perceptible factor in our lives. Then there was her aged mother-in-law, a blind crone, the Babushka of Slav legend, and the grandfather, a gnarled, ninety-year-old, who was bent double like a hook, from a life underground in the mines of Pernik. He was a great anxiety to all of us, as he invariably got on the wrong side of a tram or a Red Army lorry, when collecting his pension. And sometimes 'Uncle Bashi-Bazouk' appeared, famished and dramatic.

We found it expensive, catering for an extra seven people, or souls as they are called poetically in Slav phraseology. But there it was. What was theirs was mine too, I knew. They were devotedly loyal. And what was mine was most certainly theirs, I reflected, sometimes with impatience, seeing the refrigerator emptied night after night, as they all gathered round my kitchen table. This was called giving Raiina a helping hand.

✧　　✧　　✧

Raiina used to add to the kitchen invasion by introducing a Gypsy friend and his dancing bear. These trained bears are the large brown kind found wandering in the hills: they become

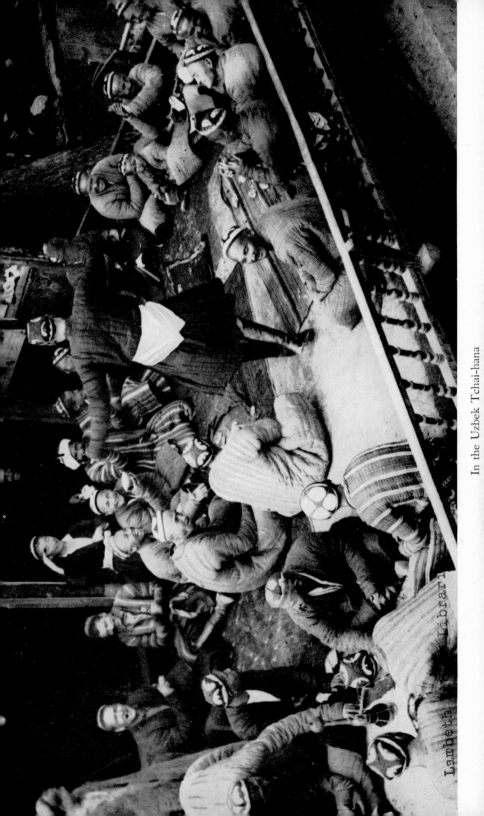

In the Uzbek Tchai-hana

A B

bum

The Queen

The Princess

The Amazon

The Mother

Mama Regina : Queen Marie of Roumania

pathetic, mangy creatures, rings through torn noses, who shuffle wearily from village to village, lumbering round in a sort of tragic dance, to the accompaniment of a zither or tambourine. They are still used as curative agents—that is, they are trained to shuffle up and down the prostrate peasants' spines, providing a sort of furry electric massage which is said to be highly tonic.

Raiina was a firm believer in the treatment, and when no bears were available (they were becoming a scarcity in Sofia) she used to adopt the substitute of a human being stamping heavily up and down her spinal column. She often fetched in a neighbour to give her a few tonic shuffles, to brace her before cooking dinner. She was fond of recounting the story of an ailing brother, to whom the bear was fetched, and, as is the custom, warmed up to its work by a tot of slivova. It seems that the creatures are partial to alcohol; it had several tots, and waxed too enthusiastic, so that Raiina's brother was in hospital for three months afterwards. Whenever we reached the point of the story where Raiina imitated the bear gulping down its fourth tot of slivova, and setting to work on her brother, she used to laugh so uproariously that the tears ran down her face. She had a strong sense of humour.

She had a strong sense of drama, too, and never missed the opportunity to wring my heart with some poignant domestic incident. If she was an hour late with breakfast, it was always because a tram had overturned, and she had been pinned underneath, en route, or it was because Minka, or Radka, or one of them, had fallen suddenly ill of a mysterious disease, and was given up for dead; detailed, but unplaceable symptoms were now accompanied by tragedienne's gestures—Minka lying on her death bed, eyes rolling upwards in a last agony '*Nyie mojie vijou*'—she could see nothing, as Raiina would say in her pidgin Bulgarian-Russian. Now it was my turn to laugh, knowing that an hour or so later, Minka would be round to the kitchen door for food, and of course, staggering under the

Raiina

weight of Borislav, who was brought to the maternal fount no less than four times a day.

When Raiina found that I could follow her stories, and that I most enjoyed the legends and customs of her birthplace, there was no stopping her. 'Ah! *Bojenka!* Ah God! my little God! if only *Gospoja* [madame] could see my Macedonia in the spring!' Then would follow a lyrical description of the mountain villages on the slopes of El Tepé. Passionately anxious to continue the conversation (cleaning and shopping bored her, she only really enjoyed cooking) she would catch me eyeing the clock and plunge into a more gripping saga of how the *smok*, or pythons, sway from the branches in the high forests—how they love milk and will come down to the pastures and hungrily crush goats and cows to death. 'Nursing mothers too', she would add, in a sinister tone, clutching her bosom. Small snakes, on the other hand, were generally considered lucky: in the nature of house-pets, or mascots. No home was really blessed if there was not a nest of these writhing terrors beside the warm hearth stones. Peasants who treated them badly were avenged by the Great Snake-Gods, she said.

Here she would become bogged in pagan legends; and descending to a more *terre à terre* level, would finish up with a last, *positively* true story. 'Ah! *Bojenka!* My little God! it happened to my own mother's sister. She had stoned a python. The great Snake-God was angry with her so he punished her cruelly. On a hot summer's day she went out picking tobacco and left her baby son asleep in its cradle, hung in the shade, under the trees. The Snake-God was watching, and he sent a little little snake into the cradle, and told it to slide into the baby's mouth while it was crying for its mother. Ah! *Gospoja!* believe me, that snake found its way straight to the baby's liver—and ate it out in two bites! Ah! *Bojenka!*,' here her voice would rise to a wail, 'It was my own child ... my little son. ...'

Proud of my linguistic progress, I would catch her out:

'But Raiina, you just said it was your mother's sister's child.'
'My *Gospoja* doesn't understand Bulgarian,' she would reply
with finality and pad back to the kitchen, where she would
throw herself on to the pastry-board in a frenzy of energy and
skill, making *banitza*, paper-thin flaked Turkish pastries
stuffed with sour cheese, to which I was partial. While cooking
such specialities she acquired all the temperamental touchiness
of a great artist. (When she was at her pastry-board, and my
husband was plunged into the writing of a complicated chapter,
the flat fairly pulsated with creative frenzies, and I often found
it advisable to go out sightseeing for the day.) Once, when I
asked her to answer the door-bell, she replied 'Anyone can
open a door—but there is only one Raiina who can make
banitza. Let them ring. Leave me in peace. . . .'

Her cooking was swayed by her passions, both political and
private. We suffered much on account of the Other Woman, a
middle-aged Gypsy matron, who used to beg from door to
door, and who was unaccountably irresistible to Raiina's
husband. Sometimes seething with fury at the Allied peace
terms laid down for Bulgaria (politics were bred in her blood
and bone, as in all her race) she was unable to produce any
meals for several days while political discussions were heard
raging in the kitchen and knives were sharpened menacingly.
Although she was, at times, an excellent cook, certain dishes
were beyond her comprehension. When first I ordered
asparagus, she cut off and threw away the heads, leaving the
white stalks, neatly stacked. *A la minute* was also outside her
grasp. In her belief that all Western Europeans were sensitive
about punctuality, she settled any question of Bulgarian
unpunctuality by having all her dishes cooked, and over-
cooking, at least two hours before the meal-times. Grilled
meat, or *shishkebab*, was always done to a turn by 11 o'clock,
and consequently quite unfit for luncheon at 1 o'clock. The
refrigerator, on the other hand, was, to her, some magic box
which freezed on sight. She was always aggrieved when,

placing a dish of hot stewed fruit inside, it was still warm ten minutes later.

Her cooking varied, too, with what she considered the social status of the guests. She had her own scale, her own hierarchy, to which she adhered rigidly. For example, Americans: to Raiina they were apart—not altogether human, and were referred to in capitals—THE AMERICANS; something about their exchange rate, the power of the dollar, the nylon stockings of the ladies, and the princely way in which the Military Mission lived in Sofia, dazzled her. The Americans, then, were fabulous, unreal: they must not be given onions, let alone garlic. The British, less fabulous but worthy of respect, must have condiments added. Mustard and pepper were great rarities at that time but, when any of the British Military Mission dined with us, flavourings were flung about lavishly. Whole avalanches of vanilla ruined the puddings; there were landslides of pepper in the soup. The other legations, she inferred, including our own the French, were not worth a spoonful of paprika. Perhaps she took the whole Corps Diplomatique with a pinch of salt.

Her family lived in great poverty, even by Shopski standards of squalor. (Shopski is the name given to peasants of the Sofia plain.) Raiina had come from a prosperous pastoral life in Macedonia; she had been a cook in many comfortable, even luxurious households, too. She liked to tell me of a former mistress who kept her elegant figure by always sleeping tightly laced into pale blue satin corsets. Raiina used to give a few graphic tugs at the imaginary laces, levering her knee against an imaginary back, to emphasize the severity of this measure. But with her marriage, there were too many children for Raiina, too many drinks for Tomislav; too little money, the old people to look after, the war, hard times. . . .

When she came to me, she was at a very low ebb. All eight of them crowded into two wretched rooms beside a garage yard near the big street market. All around were sordid slum streets where the Tziganes snored in the doorways between peddling their basket wares. The windows looked on to a coal dust heap which was speckled with refuse and filthy scraps of rag and paper. She could not find anywhere else to live.

They slept six in a room, four in a bed, until I found them some mattresses. In summer it was fiercely hot. In winter it was deadly cold, the broken windows papered over as protection against the north-easterly wind; 'Serbski wind', Raiina used to say, with hatred, expressing, meteorologically, the traditional feud between Serb and Bulgar. One night, returning late from a party and having locked ourselves out, we had to wake up Raiina for her key. It was a scene from *The Lower Depths*. After that night I understood my denuded larder.

Raiina had the primitive people's love of gossip: tom-tom quick, a piece of Corps Diplomatique scandal would cross the town and Raiina always knew it, though living, it seemed, a restricted life between our home, her own and the markets. One day, hearing blows and cries resounding through the house, I rushed into the hall where I found Raiina belabouring a bawling daughter. Minka was pretty and fourteen, and that morning she had walked home from school with a soldier; but only a few hours later, Raiina knew all about this seemingly innocent occurrence. With one last cuff she shut the door on Minka's wails. 'That'll teach her not to lose her virginity in a hurry,' she said tartly, and went back to the kitchen, where she was preparing a lethal mixture designed for the beetles, in a twin saucepan to that which contained our soup. From the purist's point of view, there is no doubt she was at fault: however delicious the yoghourt she made, her methods cut the appetite. Yoghourt must be left for twenty-four hours at an even temperature, preferably by a smouldering hearth. As our modern Sofia flat was equipped with a gas-stove and gas was in short supply, Raiina liked to meet the challenge by wrapping the bowl in a draggled flannel petticoat, which, on specially cold days, she would add to her already voluminous skirts.

Finding that I was squeamish about a number of things, she knew just how to strike back when I had been what she considered unjustly strict or unappreciative. She would accept the rebuke with no more than a reproachful glance, but a few hours later, seeing that I was particularly enjoying a Bulgarian cigarette, she would seize the occasion to remind me of the process by which such superlative tobacco was achieved. Or was achieved when, as a girl, she worked in the factory at Plovdiv. Intense heat is required during the process of preparation. The rooms where the leaves are sorted were maintained at sweltering heat. The girls, Gypsies and peasants who sorted, were drenched in sweat; the stench was overpowering. But their sweat was a vital part of the process, for it helped to ferment the tobacco rapidly, giving it a special quality. . . . As I stubbed out my cigarette, Raiina would watch me with a marked air of triumph.

❖   ❖   ❖

At one point, acting on the advice of kind friends who imagined a more orderly household could be achieved by the presence of a superior French-speaking housekeeper, a stout, granite-faced Polish lady was engaged. Mme. Euphrosnia was the widow of a Bulgarian army officer; she took over completely, and made short work of Raiina, keeping her at the housework, or running errands. Minka, Radka, Lili, Borislav and Tomislav faded out of sight, like excommunicated wraiths. Borislav was nurtured less often, and only on the service staircase. I sat in the salon in splendid isolation, and we all felt we knew our place. Matters were complicated by the fact that, after all, Mme. Euphrosnia spoke less French than I did Russian; and she found herself quite unable, or unwilling, to follow my pidgin-Bulgarian. This meant that Raiina, who never had any trouble to understand me, was constantly called in to interpret. I fancy she sometimes took liberties with my phrases, interpreting them in the light of her own attitude towards Mme. Euphrosnia, for I sometimes saw an outraged expression settle on this lady's hatchet, yet pudding, face. After a month of unbearable gentility and heavily Germanic meals Raiina was reinstated.

It was a triumphal return. When we had got back to our own ways again, and were eating yoghourt heavily laced with garlic and had time once more to discuss the heroic exploits of Christo Botiev, the legendary Bulgarian patriot, or to linger at the window watching the manège across the road, where the Horse Guards were always breaking in new recruits or new mounts; when, in fact, the former, comfortable slipshod rhythm was again established, we were able to discuss Mme. Euphrosnia with luxurious spite. But she had served her purpose. We were drawn closer by bonds of suffering: and we all appreciated each other more, afterwards.

✤   ✤   ✤

By any standards Raiina was a remarkable character; but her sensitivity and flexibility and her artistic perceptions were extraordinary, considering her background. She had a painter's eye; her taste was as instinctive and restrained as her judgements on people were shrewd. She loved to pore over the various *editions d'art* which filled our bookshelves. She was, I remember, particularly fond of Chagall's mysterious paintings. We used to stand together, watching the changing light on the far slopes of Vitosha, upon which the windows gave. Often, she would call me to the kitchen to see the reflected sunset glow on the distant range of mountains—the Balkan—which ring the plain of Sofia as far as the eye can see. She was a poetic creature: that is, she sensed, and sought for beauty.

She loved music too. Particularly the traditional folk songs and *horo* dances of her country. This was a great bond between us, as I too passionately loved their elaborate rhythms and their wildness. Some of the most beautiful of them originated in Macedonia, and these she would sing by the hour—not very well, it must be admitted. But when the nostalgic wailing chants wafted out from some neighbouring café, or on the radio, to which, on such occasions, I was glued, she would drop everything, even Borislav, and rush to find me. 'Quick *Gospoja!* the *horo* from *my* Macedonia!' Closing her eyes she would begin to shuffle and stamp. '*Gospoja!* the Ratchinitza!' she would cry and seizing my handkerchief, she was off in the rapid twirling coquettish handkerchief dance, while kettles boiled over, and telephones shrilled unanswered.

She liked to ask me about London or Paris: how the buses looked, the Tour Eiffel, the pattern of the English kitchen, my dogs, my mother. She identified herself with my family and knew a lot of extraneous details about my life. My husband's war-time career as a Free French airman attached to the R.A.F. was a favourite topic. She liked to hear over and over again about his medals and his wounds. She would nod her head. 'Tch! Tch! how sadly Our Sir has suffered,' she would say. She always spoke of him as Our Sir: *Nash Gospodin.* It had a biblical ring. To her I was *Moya Gospoja*—my madam.

She grew to know my mother's handwriting—it was a highly personal baroque kind which, however, was quite indecipherable to Raiina who could barely read and write the Kyrillic script. She would hang round me until I opened the letter and read her choice extracts. Sometimes, when she had annoyed me, I would punish her by leaving the letter unopened for some hours. This was a real torment to her. Finally she would break down and bringing me the letter once more, she would say anxiously: 'And how is Mama? Has she got over that cold? How are the cats? What does she say about Mr. Churchill?' One of my dearest remembrances of Raiina was the day when I had news that my mother was very ill, and I decided to rush back to London as soon as possible. My husband was in Belgrade at that moment, and I felt particularly low-spirited. The heating had broken down, I remember, which added to the gloom of the winter's afternoon with the snow banked outside, and the 'Serbski wind' howling down from the mountains. Raiina made me sit in the kitchen with her while she baked wonderful rich biscuits for me to take to my mother (this was her idea of a restorative) and between bouts of baking she insisted on warming my frozen feet in the oven, while she sang me, for the hundredth time, the mysterious, unknown *Lilac-bleeding Star*.

And now the moment had come. Now, at last Raiina comforted and rewarded me with the legend she had so long withheld, the legend I found so intriguing. In Macedonia they say that those with a wanderlust, who tear up their roots, betray their true-love and desert their homes because they long for faraway lands, are born under a Lilac-bleeding Star. It leads them on, and weeps for them, its tears, the lilac sparks that glitter in a winter sky . . .

'*Your* star, *Gospodja*,' says Raiina, mournfully, knowing that one day I shall leave Bulgaria for ever, leave her, leave the people and the place I love so much, tearing up more roots, tearing out some more of my heart, because I too was born under the Lilac-bleeding Star.

Our relationship was often strained. Sometimes, at breaking point over the accounts—arithmetic in Bulgarian—I even struck her. I do not think she bore me any malice: it was all part of the violent pattern of life in the Balkans, where blows and caresses, all equally extravagant, were daily life.

Gradually, Raiina came to assume the unique status of a family Nanny, but with an added dynamism which was endlessly intriguing. I should like to have kept her with me always, but even if I could have detached her from the country, she was too loving a mother to leave Minka, Radka, Lili and

Borislav, though I think she might have abandoned Tomislav to the Other Woman.

Before the dreaded day of my departure came, when all my life in Bulgaria was crated and packed away, I settled Raiina in another situation. But her new mistress had a dinner-party the night I left Sofia and would not give Raiina leave to come to the station. I was packing at the Legation, where I spent my last days, when she suddenly burst into my room carrying a little cake she had made for the journey. A little cake, and her photograph in Macedonian costume. We both burst into tears. I ate the cake and I have lost the photograph. But Raiina will always remain in my heart. Dear, dear Raiina.

5

The Fading Garden and the Forgotten Rose—A Balkan Queen

The little Balkan kingdoms immortalized as Ruritania or Graustark were once very real, last strongholds of those privileged monarchies that bloomed so exotically all over Europe and grew particularly fanciful as the Danube wound eastwards towards the Black Sea. Now, all over a greying world, former royal residences stand shuttered and dusty, or are put to more practical uses. Pekin's summer palace swarms with tourists; the marble halls of the Rajput maharajahs are crumbling under fierce suns. Everywhere, great gilded and mirrored perspectives echo to the shuffle of felt-slippered sightseers. The northern palaces of Tzardom have became museums; their Crimean mansions sanatoriums. The sober magnificence of Marlborough House is given over to Commonwealth Conferences. The Emir of Bokhara's summer palace and the garden of his harem, where the peacocks still trail their glories, has become a clinic for kidney complaints, starched white hospital aprons replacing the gauzy finery of the odalisques.

Perhaps the most evocative of all lesser royal residences, (apart from such monuments of self-indulgence as Linderhof, built by the mad King Ludwig of Bavaria) is the tiny summer palace, hardly larger than a pavilion, which Queen Marie of Roumania built for herself on the Black Sea coast, at Balcic, and where she was able to express the more untrammelled aspects of her temperament and imagination: where the *woman* rather than the Queen—even the superb Ruritanian Queen she was—could sometimes live entirely in the picturesque manner she favoured. However much she was photographed in peasant costumes, with richly patterned aprons, a weaving shuttle in her hand, her preference was, in fact, for something more exotic. By the time she built Balcic her taste had crystallized, and the little villa was, like her style of dresses, a highly personal blend of Byzantine luxury and a note of unmistakably Elinor Glyn romanticism.

This queenly retreat was still much discussed in the People's Balkans, when we arrived there, in 1946. Many of the peasants still clung to the after-glow of Royalty, while the Party condemned it, but both were intrigued. The royal pavilion assumed a legendary quality, like the stately pleasure dome that Kublai Khan decreed. During the Queen's life-time it had been scarcely less legendary, being shrouded in mystery and in-nuendo. Only the most privileged ever penetrated there. But eight years after the Queen's death—after World War II and the establishment of another way of life, the Roumanian Government used to lend it, on occasions, to those they favoured. Anyone who visited the place always returned with lively descriptions of its octagonal room with the alcove bed. I grew tired of hearing how various high-ranking Allied generals, chiefs of missions and ministers all slept well there—loved the bathing—the boating—the shooting—the Gypsy music. . . . None of them heard its echoes, or made more than a casual reference to the woman, whose turbulence and majesty had stirred even the Balkans, and who had conceived the little palace as her refuge from reality: for even Ruritania had its own brand of such.

✣   ✣   ✣

This pavilion, or folly, and the larger but less imaginative Château of Euxinograd (*faux* French-Renaissance, turreted and pompous) which was built by a neighbouring ruler, the Tzar Ferdinand of Bulgaria were places we came to know well while *en poste* in Sofia. Both were haunted houses, haunted by phantoms of princes and privilege.

Euxinograd is a pin-point on the map. There is no village, but the little *plage*, or private bathing beach belonging to the château has one end of its sickle scoop emphasized by a miniature jetty and lighthouse. The *plage*, though that is perhaps too worldly a name for so unpretentious a shore, was still private property when we were there, being then reserved for high-ranking Party members, or Bulgarian Government officials. In 1946 the Allied Control Commission was still in being in Bulgaria, and the military missions and legations had requisitioned villas all along the coast, while some of the Corps Diplomatique, ourselves among them, were able to taste the paradisiacal delights of both Euxinograd and Balcic.

Euxinograd was Arcadia and Ruritania in one. The tiny bay was backed by cliffs tangled in tropic vegetation, and sloping, by way of the palmy, still perfectly trimmed royal gardens, to vineyards edging down on to the sands, so that it was possible to reach up out of the water and pick a bunch of enormous, egg-sized grapes which are said to yield a particularly fragrant white wine. Looking inland from the jetty, the fluffily wooded coast, sparsely dotted with villas was rather as the French Riviera must have been in its far away, uncorrupted past. In the middle of the white sand beach stood a ridiculously ornate little wooden pavilion, an orange painted chalet, divided into six or seven cabins, where once the royal bathers used to shuffle in and out of their clothes. A narrow gangplank, with stout hand rails, ran down to the sea, but it was rusted and rotting now, half buried in the loose sand.

I imagined the Tzar Ferdinand and his Ruritanian Court, frisking down it to the water's edge, 'Foxy Ferdi' to his detractors, his tiny ferret eyes set too close to his far too long nose, smiling his curiously sly smile as he led his guests, in a barrel-striped bathing suit, his plump, white, over-manicured fingers for once bare of the precious stones he loved with such oriental abandon. I saw the ladies of the party dressed up for their dip, in black stockings and mackintosh mob-caps, bobbing up and down, keeping their pink and white complexions and tong-waved coiffures high and dry, while shrieking and simpering in the shallows.

But these are tougher times. We used to lie on the sand, baking ourselves to crackling, watching a party of lean, black-brown Bulgarians; the men in their tiny loincloths, the women with a bandana handkerchief brassière added, as they swam far out to sea, the flail-like precision of the crawl stroke churning the dark blue water.

Perched half-way up the cliff, there was a little gazebo, a ruined summer-house, with trellised arches, and a thatched roof. We used to pause there, as we climbed the path on our way home, at sunset. The lilac bushes almost hid it from the path: there were old cobwebs, with dead wasps entangled, and sometimes a snake slithered away as we approached. Sitting there, looking through the lattice-work at the fading blue of the sea, and the tiny dots which were fishermen's boats, still out after the few fish which live in this part of the Black Sea, I used to think again of the little Ruritanian Court which had vanished.

No doubt the summer-house was a favourite rendezvous for those complicated picnic teas beloved of the Edwardians and their contemporaries. I imagined the paraphernalia; the parasols and cushions, the royal ladies and their ladies-in-waiting in tussore dustcoats, buttoned boots and enormous hats with tulle veils which they furled on to the bridge of their rice-powdered nose preparatory to sipping tea. There would be gentlemen—plenty of gentlemen—with whom to flirt, for in that world, few worked except at pleasure. The gentlemen would be wearing white flannels, blazers and straw boaters, or panama hats, for one still dressed formally out of doors. They would be very highly born ... the younger Russian grand dukes, a smattering of Hapsburgs, Hungarian nobles and the German princelings, Saxe-Meiningens, Coburgs and Hesses, a stock which peopled the courts of Europe, bringing their blazons and their hereditary taints to each fresh alliance.

While panting footmen staggered along the cliff paths with picnic baskets filled with an elaborate tea, cucumber sandwiches and puffed-up pâtisseries and spirit lamps and sugar tongs and lace napkins and all the fiddle-de-dee of the drawing-room, there would be a lot of tittle-tattle within the perimeter of the *Almanach de Gotha*. Once in a while a lady would glance down over the still blue bay and someone would be sure to say it was just the colour of her eyes. And then, someone else would light a cigarette, a perfumed Balkan cigarette, held in a pale, kid-gloved hand, gloved, even in Arcadia.

O! gazebo, thy name is nostalgia! All over Europe the gazebos and arbours of past dalliance are ruins, now: memorials to an irresponsible, yet charming way of life—charming for those who lived it, that is. Charming for Great Catherine, 'the Semiramis of the North', lying in her favourite's arms, in a Chinese pagoda, at Tzarskoe Selo; for the aristos in the Hameau at the Petit Trianon; for Charles II and his zenana of beauties, as he moored a State barge-load of them beside the landing-stage at Hampton Court.

A mixture of Paul Pry-ism and tourist zeal made us accept an invitation to visit Balcic. The town, we heard, was nothing special—a few fishing boats, a squalid Gypsy *mahalla* or settlement, and a few modern villas: but there was Queen's Folly. We left Euxinograd on a lambent August morning, and drove east, into the fierce sun, mounting the hairpin bends which connect one great tableland with the next in a series of slab-like plateaux. This is the Dobrudja: chalky wastes, white dust, white oxen, sheep and a blinding blue sky. There are great plains, dotted with dusty scrub, and many miles of giant sunflowers with heads like lolling dinner-plates. They are grown for their oil; the seeds, or semki, are the Slav equivalent of chewing gum. We stopped to pick some, and went on our way chewing, crossing the old Roumanian frontier, a sort of Balkan Maginot line, sunken fortifications and camouflaged gun-turrets embedded in white rocks.

The Dobrudja has always been a bone of contention between Bulgaria and Roumania; it has always been fought over, ceded by one treaty and retracted by another. There is a wild ad-mixture of races here, Turks, Gagaoutz and Tartars. The Gagaoutz are centred in this part of the Dobrudja; they were always very much favoured by the Turks, who considered the whole area, particularly the great forest of Deli Orman, to be a natural frontier defence against the Russians.

In Turkish, Deli Orman means 'The Mad Wood'. Nothing could be better named. The huge tracts of forest—flat forest—sprawl across the plain. The trees writhe in a never-ceasing wind which howls round them by day and night, winter or summer, a restless, maddening wind blowing straight from the steppes, before it rages on, to cross the Black Sea, strike the shores of Turkey and whip the waters of the Bosphorus.

✳   ✳   ✳

The little town of Balcic is reached by a sudden descent, through lime-stone crags. It lies basking at the foot of the cliffs, sheltered from tempests, and indeed, from life itself. It is quite improbable, having a toy-like quality, as if designed as a backcloth for Mr. Pollock's celebrated *Juvenile Drama*, the 'Penny Plain and Two Pence Coloured' sheets which enchanted Victorian children. Act II Scene 3. A Pirates' Port on the Illyrian Coast. Ramshackle, doll-sized houses, pink and blue and yellow, cling to the cliffs giddily. The miniature harbour, with its *douane*, shop and inn are set down between perpen-dicular white crags and hummocks looking like toy volcanoes. Lemon and fig trees burst from the fissures. One or two over-ornamented but cardboard-like buildings, the town hall among them, are pressed against the rocks in tiers, and there are a couple of blue-domed Orthodox churches and a little mosque with coloured-glass lozenges to trim its windows. Everything seemed to come out of a box of children's bricks.

On the cliffs above we found clots of shack dwellings and the ever-irresistible *mahalla* where the Gypsies live; the women in ragged chintz trousers toned down to a faint pastel by the all-pervading white dust. They squatted on their haunches searching their children's heads intently, while the children, a beautiful and dissipated-looking lot, picked ticks off the heaving flanks of the sheep which were tethered by every door. At a haughty distance we saw a line of modern luxury villas, once owned by the rich Roumanians who used to follow their Queen's lead and flock to Balcic in the summer. But they were standing shuttered and empty now. Turning our steps towards another abandoned dwelling, we left the pretty paste-board town and followed a road beside the cliff, towards Queen Marie's summer palace . . . the legend we had come to see.

✤   ✤   ✤

It is no secret that the Queen built this villa as an amorous retreat. Her heart was buried in the Byzantine chapel by the lily garden. In spite of all its highly coloured implications, and the exoticism of its architecture and setting (near-Turkish), this royal folly retains a muted, tomb-like quality. But the loneliness, so apparent to us now, was, I believe, always there, echoing, along with self-conscious voluptuousness, some melancholy strain of the Queen's own nature. Although she was generally surrounded by adulation, she remained, in herself, an exile; from that overwhelming love she craved; from her English background, and from the pomp and power which was also her birthright, and which she only achieved to a much lesser degree in her adopted country. These undercurrents of sadness, of regret and a quality of defiant bravery are apparent throughout her Memoirs. They are a remarkable achievement, quite certainly her own; they bear no traces of the ghost-writer's sickly hand, so abundantly evident in other autobiographies of high-born personages. Her portraits are brilliant; she sees very clearly for one of her rank; it is 'Missy' the unconventional Englishwoman writing, rather than a queen. Even when describing her children, she retains her penetrating judgement; Elizabeth, a silent, cold child with steel-strong little hands, not perhaps a sympathetic character; Mignon, like a full-blown peony, easy-going, loving, and giving, 'one of those luminous bridges back to hope, which are given to us occasionally . . . after great darkness . . .'. Carol, the Crown Princeling, at once taken away from her to be brought up by others; brought up wrong. And Ileana, the angel child. 'If Mignon was the child of my flesh, Ileana was certainly the child of my soul.' She is a passionately loving mother, but she is not blinded; she is a queen, her children must share the burdens of monarchy. It is said that during the last stormy days of King Carol II's rule, when a bitter quarrel with his brother Prince Nicolas brought them to the shooting-point, the Queen Mother rushed between her sons, flung her body across that of Carol, the King and so, stopping the bullet believed she had saved the monarchy. But it was lost, one way or another, and she herself never fully recovered from the wound.

Two great rulers were her grandparents, Queen Victoria on her father's side; the Tzar Alexander II, 'the Liberator', on her mother's side. As Queen of a newly formed, insignificant Balkan country she felt faintly déclassée. She was irresistibly beautiful, illustriously born . . . a great catch among the royal princesses. Yet she was married off at sixteen, since her mother, the Duchess of Edinburgh, believed any royal crown, however small, was preferable to a mere ducal one; 'Princesses must be married off young, otherwise they begin to think for themselves', was one of her beliefs. She herself had not been happy in her marriage; as the only daughter of the mighty Tzar Alexander II, she had felt keenly her loss of prestige at the British Court; she had detested what seemed to her its middle-class aspects; she spent much time abroad, wearing dull clothes, the magnificent jewels of her dowry unused; her only link with the barbaric splendour of her youth were the glittering ikons which adorned her rooms, and the rich vestments of the priest and two chanters who followed her everywhere to maintain the mystic rituals of her Orthodox faith.

Her three daughters adored her and were in awe of her too. She allowed them a singularly unrestricted childhood . . . and then all of a sudden it was time to marry. She found herself betrothed to Ferdinand, 'Nando', a shy young Hohenzollern-Sigmaringen prince, heir apparent to the Roumanian throne then occupied by his uncle, King Carol I. King George V, then an inconsiderable young naval prince at Malta, under the command of the Duke of Edinburgh's squadron, had fallen a victim to the charms of Missy, the little Princess who rode and romped with him, but he was not taken seriously, he was only a second son; the English throne seemed remote. Who could have foreseen then that his elder brother, the Duke of Clarence, would die suddenly and he would find himself Heir Apparent? At sixteen 'Missy' became the Crown Princess of Roumania, and George, the Duke of York, married Princess May of Teck. Together they lived a long life of public glory and private happiness. But for all that it was known that 'May' never quite forgave 'Missy' for having been her husband's special weakness. Such beauty as Missy's always caused pangs all round.

Queen Marie's ambitions grew to match the extravagance of her Ruritanian setting. She came to see herself as a Byzantine Empress figure, ruling over the entire Balkans; her dream, that of 'UNIRE' . . . unity, the wild dream of Roumanian patriots, scheming a Balkanic empire, Bulgaria, Serbia, Macedonia, Albania ... all the territories stretching from Turkey to Austria, and all under her Roumanian rule. After the death of King Ferdinand, when King Carol relinquished his kingdom, a Council of Regency was to be appointed; two elder statesmen, the Patriarch and her anointed self. It was her hour of triumph. To become one with her people, she had been converted to the Orthodox faith, and now she would grasp that power which had eluded her during her long apprenticeship as Crown Princess, and which, during her husband's reign, had not been as absolute as she desired. Her intentions were noble: she had become, over the years, an ardent patriot, a large-minded, courageous woman, a leader who had upheld her country magnificently in the years of battle and stress. But to many she remained the outsider: the Englishwoman, the frivolous beauty, the sorceress, the intriguer. . . . Even her conversion to the Orthodox faith did not win over her detractors.

At the very hour when she was donning her robes of state, and all the veils and diadems and cordons by which she dramatized her official appearances, her enemies were denouncing her at the Parliament and invoking Salic law. Messengers rushed to the palace to warn her ... it was impossible that after such an attack, she could be sworn in. Once again, absolute power had eluded her. Her disappointment was tragic, her fury unbridled. I have heard it said that she flung herself on the ground, rolling backwards and forwards in paroxysms of rage, her jewels scattered, her robes torn. Her Romanov blood seethed and overboiled; her quieter, more stubborn English reactions, which had sustained her through so many years of strife, were temporarily overcome and both gave place to purely Balkanic violence.

This story, like so many others centred round the Queen, may be apocryphal; those who circulated it pursed their lips, as they so often did, discussing her unpredictable actions. . . .

Yet, regrettable, violent, . . . whatever they called it, it was in keeping with this figure, so much larger than life, in all her life-force, her beauty and daring. She was a queen who had come to identify herself with her adopted country and to assume not only the more theatrical aspects of the Crown, which such a people understood, but also to express her emotions in their uninhibited manner.

Great queens—and in her age and setting I think she was such—have a way of epitomizing their country. She herself was aware of this. In her Memoirs, writing of the successive coronations of King Edward VII, her uncle, and King George V, her cousin, at Westminster Abbey she emphasizes in each case, the sense of sober, unquestioning magnificence.

> The Queens' faces were severe, almost unmoved, the thrones they were mounting were, if I can so express it, seats of peace. . . . Queen Alexandra and Queen Mary: two serene figures . . . their crowns, although weighted by a hundred gems, did not seem to oppress them . . . there was an established security about these Queens which made you feel glad for them, not afraid!

In contrast, in prophetic contrast, she saw her cousin the Tzar Nicholas II crowned in the Kremlin; beside him, the doomed Tzarina,

> the young Empress—standing rigidly upright, her golden robes flowing from her shoulders, her face flushed, her eyes tragic, her lips tightly set as though at bay.

If queens reflect the character of their country, no two better examples of Balkan romanticism, of a sort of stylized monarchy could be found, than Queen Marie and her predecessor, Queen Elizabeth, widely known as the poetess Carmen Sylva. By the time the Crown Princess Marie became Queen, in 1914, she had evolved her own style—Byzantine—but Carmen Sylva had been Wagnerian. Both were generally swathed in innumerable veils and indeterminate draperies. Both these ladies saw themselves as figureheads—symbols of monarchy. They were, each in their own way, *monstres sacres*. Both were 'artistic,' wrote poetry, painted, were musicians and fostered the beautiful peasant arts of Roumania. But whereas Carmen Sylva was intense, and had no gleam of humour, Queen Marie was able to laugh at everything, including herself—except over the matter of her clothes—and here, perhaps she was influenced by her wish to provide the peasant majority with a figure-head in their own terms.

To be royal was to be, in a sense, theatrical: whether she believed, like her ancestors, in the divine right of kings or whether she moved with the times and sensed the growing artificiality of the metier, she dressed the part. Besides, she frankly liked dressing-up. With each change of costume she revealed another aspect or mood. The Princess in her Carpathian castle, shadowy pillared halls, divans piled with bearskins, walls hung with rare ikons, and the Queen, splendid in her trailing robes and jewels, enthroned among her courtiers and admirers. The fairy-tale Roumanian Princess visiting her remote provinces on a shaggy pony, wearing top-boots and embroidered aprons, who will wave her wand, put on her golden crown and right all the wrongs. The lovely and fecund mother, joy of the dynasty, in a tea-gown, all softness, surrounded by her beautiful brood; the mature woman, the Mother Queen, Mama Regina to her soldiers, in a nurse's uniform, at the front in the hospitals—and here she was playing no part, but was flung into the tragic ordeals of her country, sharing, retreating, upholding with selfless devotion.

In 1916, when everything seemed lost for Roumania, there was a question of exile, of forming a Roumanian colony in Kharkov, Poltava, or some other Russian province. She was aghast. Her country had become her life. 'This would mean complete exile', she writes in her journal. 'The thought is so utterly ghastly that one accepts it quietly, without words of complaint or protest, as one accepts the thought of death.'

But she went on fighting furiously. And here she was

playing no rôle, and needed no carefully devised costume. Her loathing of the German enemy was intense. Many of her relatives were Germans; her husband's sympathies and training had been as Germanic as his blood, and that of his predecessor, the old King Carol. She was the Roumanian, among them all. Perhaps her Russian ancestry helped her to love and understand the Balkans: something wild in her responded to its own wildness. In the mountains, she is remembered as an Amazon— she was unmatched as a horsewoman—galloping across tracks few could follow, riding astride, mounted on a wild Cossack horse, gift of a Russian admirer, and wearing a Circassian uniform (sent by another enslaved Slav), a dark-blue caftan braided with silver, over a scarlet under-tunic, silver cartouchières across the chest, and a dagger at her then very slim waist. She describes herself as an over-picturesque apparition. But how pleasing to both player and public. She was undoubtedly narcissistic—delighted with herself—but not self-satisfied. There is a great difference.

That style which might be described as basic Balkan Royal, veils and trailing draperies, which were, in a sense, Queen Marie's trademark, spread from one Balkan kingdom to the next. Her two elder daughters became respectively Queens of Greece and Yugoslavia, and followed the Roumanian tradition, floating about their own realms, similarly draped, the apotheosis of queendom. (It was left to their youngest sister, the Princess Ileana, married to an Austrian archduke and mother of a large family, to face life in exile in America, doing the housework uncomplaining, in tweeds.) But in the last afterglow of royal radiance before World War II, newsreels and press photographs recording great occasions east of the Danube were immediately recognizable, not so much by some distinguishing cathedral or monument, as by the trailing toilettes of the three queens. These bore no relation to fashion, nor indeed, did those equally stylized but less emotional costumes which Queen Alexandra and Queen Mary of England evolved. But all of them, in their own way, knew that the mystique of Royalty must be fostered by every means, and that a queen must have everything to do with pure style, and nothing to do with mere fashion; still less, must a monarchy appear middle-class.

Even in her dying Queen Marie displayed that dramatic sense which lit her life. She had been born to the purple, and she asked that for her funeral Bucharest would be hung with purple rather than black. Thus the banal streets through which the cortège passed assumed a drama and beauty, draped in violet, lilac and the Byzantine purple she had always craved.

❖   ❖   ❖

Queen Marie loved and knew well the peasants; she did not make rounds of scheduled royal visits so much as a series of personal, impulsive, sorties among them; into their villages and houses, accompanied by one lady-in-waiting rather than a suite, or perhaps only one of her daughters, talking to the people in her broken Roumanian which always made them smile, but her heart going out to them in a manner they understood. She had, in fact, the common touch, without the patronage which that implies. She would appear unexpectedly in a village, share a peasant's meal with relish, discuss their crops and their hopes, listen to their legends, and allow herself to be, literally, taken to their ragged and often noisome bosoms. To such people she was never remote, though among the court she could quell at a glance, as she could charm. Writing of a pair of old crones, 'my two old witches', she relates being dragged into their arms and their quarrels. To the peasants she was always 'Mama Regina'. 'Your tiny dried up little heart is black as sin,' spat one witch to the other, then pointing to the Queen, 'but Mama Regina's heart is round and red and full of love.'

This was the sort of compliment she valued most, as she

preferred the armfuls of wildflowers the ragged children brought her to all the formal bouquets with which her path was strewn. With the years, she and her husband had drifted far apart; 'Nando' had once been, as she says, 'almost cruelly in love' ... but they always remained united in their patriotism and their passion for flowers. Nando was something of a botanist; they both flung themselves into gardening, and both continued to bring each other flowers of all kinds, marvelling at them, together, till the last.

✣   ✣   ✣

In her early days in Bucharest the Princess had been pathetically lonely, cut off, in a strange setting, among strangers, very far from home, surrounded by rigid etiquette, a never-ending round of stern duties, of constraint, and criticism; but as she grew to sense her power as a Princess, as a beautiful woman, and to sense too the special flavour of her new country, she, sometimes showed an almost outrageous exuberance. Her craving for pleasure, sterner Court circles said, was dangerous in one so near the throne. It was a German-held throne, painfully earnest and austere and quite out of touch with the Roumanian national temperament. King Carol I, 'Der Onkel' to the young Crown Prince and Princess, had his hands full striving to raise the European status of his small kingdom, and to inculcate his own strict standards, first to his eccentric wife, Carmen Sylva, and then to his nephew and heir's wife, the Princess Marie. It was grudgingly admitted that she worked tirelessly at her duties, but she *would* dance till dawn ... then dash off on one of those wild horses that only she could ride. She *would* know the most unsuitable people ... painters, musicians, that fast international set, the Plesses, and all those Russian grand dukes ... (cousins, but still ...) True she was giving the nation a whole nursery full of splendid little princes and princesses ... But she had some *giddy* strain ... driving along the Chauseé Kissileff at sunset! . . . (this was Bucharest's Bois de Boulogne, the elegant promenade for *monde* and *demi-monde* alike). Not for our Crown Princess, said the critics, watching her open carriage bowl past as she smiled and bowed with that almost childish glee, her chic feathered or flowered hat framing those enormous blue eyes that worked such havoc. She wrote fairy stories, painted, built herself a house in the treetops, explored the street markets of Bucharest for antiques . . . it was all very unconventional. And then she *would* summon the Lauteri to her parties. They were the Gypsies whose hot-blooded violins were legendary, but particularly *mal vue* by the Court. Yet somehow they were always around, their emotional strains undermining Royal fanfares.

Her giddiness, like her loneliness, is all recorded with remarkable objectivity in her Memoirs. But in the last volume, with the outbreak of the first world war, another depth, or dimension, is revealed. She has grown up, at last. Her country's desperate needs, as it was slowly abandoned, overcome, and fought back to victory, makes heroic reading. She does not spare us, as she did not spare herself. In Indian heat and Russian cold, which are the extremes of the Roumanian climate, she knew no rest. She was all over the country, wherever she could be of use. Beside the troops, retreating, in field hospitals where dead and wounded were piled on the mud-floored huts sanded over with lice; at headquarters, everywhere, she toiled day and night, with ferocity of purpose and tenderness of spirit, lashing at the politicians who dared speak of submission, or defeat; at a base hospital, feeding, for want of anything else, spoonfuls of jam to the gaunt soldiers. In the midst of disease, famine, and typhus epidemics she refuses to wear gloves ('They all want to kiss my hand . . . how can I ask them to kiss india-rubber?') Her journal records this terrible time as she battles on, fighting fatigue, despair, and lice too. And still her extraordinary animal vitality asserts itself. She enjoys, sensuously, the sight of a lime tree in flower; or a packet of ginger biscuits, conjuring the far-away securities of an English tea-table on the lawn at Osborne, with Grandmama Queen.

But this is no time for nostalgia. Her tears are kept for memories of Mircea, 'my little Mircea', the baby who died at the beginning of the war, and whose grave she has had to leave untended when, with the King and the army, she retreats before the enemy. The thought of the lonely little grave torments her unceasingly. She goes to church, 'I wept, as only a broken-hearted mother can weep, the mother of a dead child, of dead hopes, the mother of a suffering people she has learned to love. . . .' She organizes Prince Mircea canteens for the starving children, sends her elder daughters, the Princesses Elizabeth and Marie 'Mignon' off to work wherever they can help. Mignon is a humble worker: she will clean windows, sweep floors or hold a leg steady for amputation with the same self-effacing zeal. The King and the Crown Prince Carol are with the armies, her other two children Nicolas and Ileana are too small to do more than accompany her on some of her tours, but they can keep up the people's morale, and she does not shield them from horrors. Except for Ileana, her children are not of her mettle or stamina; Elizabeth collapses at one point, Marie at another; then Nicolas, and we sense her impatience . . . the exasperation of a very strong woman who cannot will others to her own degree of endurance. Perfect health and a good digestion 'my Russian digestion' as she describes it gratefully, sustained her through ordeals that felled others. But she had her courage; it runs like a thread of challenge throughout her life. And always, at all times, she is fiercely unresigned.

All around her are horrors. 'A long long day dark with pain and revolt', she writes, as they fall back again. Every retreat is also measured by her heart, for its distance from Mircea's lonely grave. One among thousands now. 'We begin to speculate in which way we are to die', she writes, knowing that for her there can never be any thought of escape. Roumania is her life.

She is photographed now in Red Cross uniform, standing defiantly, in contrast to the more soothing poses generally struck by other Royal ladies in other afflicted countries. While they are folding bandages, or visiting tidied-up bedsides, she is at clearing stations, where the wounded shriek and die. Unshrinking, she washes open the eyes of a shattered face, one last look of gratitude her reward, and torment. There are no more hospitals, no more guns, no more support from Russia, for the giant is collapsing in chaos and betrayal. Treachery is everywhere, even at home.

Disbanded Russian troops straggle across Roumania's ravaged land, and are now only so many more mouths to feed. The pro-German clique is strong around the King, himself of German origin. The Queen is uncompromisingly pro-British, pro-French, pro-Allied. As granddaughter of 'the Tzar Liberator' she is half Russian. The Russian debâcle appalls her. 'Nicky' abdicates at Mohilev. She knows him weak, a disastrous ruler, overpowered by Alix, whom she cannot like; but the abdication is, to her, betrayal of a sacred trust. No news comes out of Russia, now; as the Revolution takes hold, all is conjecture and rumour. She is anguished for news of her sister 'Duckie', wife of the Grand Duke Cyrill Vladimirovitch. The Red flag is hoisted over his palace in St. Petersburg, for at first he is in sympathy with any movement which will silence the Tzarina, 'the German woman', in her rôle as dictator and mouthpiece for the monk Rasputin.

In Roumania the war drags on. The soldiers have no soles to their boots, now: no more guns, no more hope. Soon Roumania is abandoned by her Allies, and the Germans take possession. In August 1918, comes news that 'Nicky' and 'Alix' and their children have been killed at Ekaterinburg. There had been a moment, before the war, when it was hoped a marriage would be arranged between Prince Carol and the

Grand Duchess Olga: the Russians made this flattering suggestion, but the young people showed no enthusiasm for each other, and the matter dropped.

Roumania falls under German rule, and the Queen suffers torments of despair and humiliation. All the high offices in the country are held by her enemies, led by the pro-German Marghiloman. In September, she receives another blow. The Crown Prince Carol betrays his country, and his heritage, in her eyes, by crossing the frontier to Odessa, and marrying clandestinely, Mademoiselle Zizi Lambrino, a commoner.

For Mama Regina this is a crushing defeat: but she is as fiercely unresigned as ever, and putting aside her personal tragedy, still opposes every hateful measure of the Marghiloman Government, still stands as a rallying-point of patriotism.

And still, she fights for beauty. She is a *force de la nature*; sun, air, flowers, laughter, children, love, and beauty are still her aura. She is exhausted by her war-time struggles, and takes a few weeks off, now, to recuperate in a simple little wooden châlet in the forest, at Cotŏfănesti. But she cannot rest until she has contrived colour and harmony around her. An old ikon and some Gypsies' brass cooking pots filled with wild-flowers help, but still craving a focal point of colour she dyes a bath towel orange and drapes it over the table. Even here, at this moment, she is still setting the stage. Those who criticized her for theatricality should recall that it was, rather, an innate sense of beauty—her own, and that of her surroundings: and when there were no luxuries, no Byzantine extravaganzas, she still created her own ambience out of nothing—or a packet of dye.

She always loved to express herself through rooms and houses. She had many. She had pined in the dark, heavy Germanic-Royal Palace where she was sequestered in the early days of her marriage. But when at last she burst from the chrysalis, she was able to create Ruritanian splendours at Cotroceni, and Peleşor, both turreted castles in the romantic Balkan tradition. Then there was the Foişor, a small forest house at Sinaia, and an odd tree-top abode, a fairy-tale hut rocking in the pines, where astonished visitors found themselves struggling up ladder-like steps for a picnic tea served in flower cups painted by the Princess. Cotrocenis' Ruritanian overtones, bearskins, ikons, Romanesque arches and pillared halls were very different to Bicaz, near Jassy, the Royal family's headquarters during the war, a thick-walled, low white building in the traditional style of a Roumanian country house. And lastly, there was Bran and Balcic, her most loved house. It was an amalgam of all her life; and then, too, it affirmed Roumania's repossession of the Dobrudja; it was an emblem of victory, and sovereignty, as well as a romantic retreat. Balcic reflected the country at its most exotic, and it was her own personal interpretation of romance. It was very far from the Court and its intrigues, but it breathed secrecy . . . a house for lovers meetings; yet I was told by one who had known it as her guest, that it always retained an air of indefinable magnificence: it was a Queen's lair.

But to me, seeing it now, abandoned, or worse, inhabited by passing strangers, it was indeed a tomb, a last monument to Ruritanian queens and high adventure. As I sat on the Queen's loggia, watching the evening sky yellowing, the swallows wheeling round the minaret, I resented my own presence there, as the intrusion it was. The gardens were still kept up, much as the Queen had planned them. At every turn there were picturesque vistas; ornamental terraces, Romanesque cloisters, and Turkish fountains. Winding paths skirted grottoes and semi-secret nooks, and led to a venerable chestnut tree reefed by chains and hanging out at a right angle over the cliffs. In its green shade stood a white marble Byzantine throne, beside it a low table made from a truncated Roman column. 'Her Majesty's favourite seat for coffee', said the caretaker, a boldly handsome black-eyed man who had followed me to this ghost-ridden terrace.

At a discreet distance from the main house, and deep in sub-tropical vegetation were several cottages, unseen but for their chimneys, peeping from the foliage like rabbits' ears, hidden but alert. These, said the caretaker, had been for the resident masseuse, hairdresser, and dressmaker. I recalled the Empress Elizabeth of Austria, whose sartorial exigencies required two tailors to sew her into her riding habit every morning. No doubt Queen Marie's trailing draperies were less demanding, but even so I fancy a resident dressmaker must have been a necessity rather than a luxury.

Dotted about the gardens were other establishments for the Queen's children, who by the time she built Balcic were all old enough to be fully appreciative of her initiative. Princess Ileana, her favourite child, had a simple little house beside the mill race. Prince Nicolas, a rather streamlined *atelier de luxe* further along the cliffs. But I doubt if King Carol and Madame Lupescu were ever lodged in the Queen Bee's hive. However romantic her view of life, Queen Marie retained an even stronger belief in the Monarchy. Nothing, no weakness of body or spirit, must ever be allowed to jeopardize the Crown, and her son's second romantic lapse was a betrayal of her whole life's purpose. That she was equally aware of the mystical, practical, and theatrical aspects of her calling are revealed in many passages of her Memoirs. In particular, writing of her accession, describing the scene in Parliament, standing beside the new King, her husband, and smothered in mourning veils for the dead monarch . . .

Suddenly my name rang through space;
'Regina Maria . . .
Regina Maria . . .!'
Then I knew I must bare my face before the whole house, that I must turn towards them with no veil of mourning between them and myself . . . 'Regina Maria!' . . . And we faced each other, my

people and I. And that was *my* hour . . . mine . . . an hour it is not given to many to live.

✤ ✤ ✤

'Did the Queen often come here?' I asked the caretaker, who was still hanging around eyeing me speculatively.

'As often as she could. She loved it here,' he replied, 'when she fell ill the doctors said it was no good for her by the sea. They said she must go to the mountains. It broke her heart to leave. She never came back. She wanted to die *here* . . . but she told them to bury her heart here, beside the chapel. It's been taken away now, though. . . . Change . . . change . . . nothing's the same, except the flowers. . . .'

He snipped the heads off some dead marigolds, and stared at me again, his dark eyes bold and questioning.

'You are interested in the Queen? You are English, as she was? You never knew her? But you like this place . . . the others who come here . . .', he shrugged, 'they only want to see the bedroom. . . .'

'Her Majesty used to watch the sunsets from the minaret,' he volunteered, 'there's a little staircase leading up beside her bedroom . . . the moon will be up before the sun is down . . . you should go up to the minaret,' and offering me a handful of dried sunflower seeds, he lounged off, chanting some sad-sounding song.

The minaret was no doubt a merely secular, or architectural concession to the locale, having no religious significance, and being more in the nature of a look-out, or a setting for moon-light tête-à-têtes. I went into the house, so disarmingly small and simple in form. There are only three rooms; a big dining- or living-room, very Ruritanian-Elinor Glyn, and above, an octagonal bedroom with windows on five sides, jutting out towards the Black Sea. Beside it are dressing rooms and a domed white marble Turkish bath-house. The celebrated bed is on a dais in an alcove. There is a hooded fireplace, flanked by fine candelabra. Firelight, starlight and candlelight . . . a frame for loving. I climbed the tiny stone stairway to the minaret, and reaching the little balcony, surveyed the beautiful and muted domain below where the shadows were gathering. In the limpid evening sky one star joined a crescent moon; it was indeed the frame for love, as the Queen would have wished it.

But is the frame enough? I fancy that when we have achieved the experience, the abandon, necessary to appreciate such a setting, we are too late; we have forgotten that the sort of love we seek does not require a frame. It is come-by-chance, born of the moment. Perhaps today's brisk matings, a kiss beside the collective tractor, and no emotional dalliance, is more real. I thought again of the departed Queen, the romantic figure whose ideals and setting time at last betrayed.

> Away with Persian pomps and fineries,
> And wreaths on linden withies nicely wound,
> Search not the fading garden
> For one forgotten rose.*

* Edward Marsh; translation of an Horatian Ode.

6

Always Travel Heavy

'Travel light' is one of those respected, age-old maxims that collapse in the face of reality, along with clichés like 'blood is thicker than water' (which takes no account of those inter-family feuds so much more ferocious than any others) or 'there's no place like home', a phrase which has a bitter ring to the harassed housewife, whose dream existence is, of course, care-free hotel living. 'Always travel light', was not, as might be expected, a slogan coined by the airlines. It began long, long before, in the ample days of rail and boat travel, when muscular porters, as amiable as husky, were waiting in ranks to fling themselves on as much luggage as one cared to bring.

Even in this day of few porters, fewer taxis, and all the stress of travel, what is described as 'care-free travelling', I have come to the conclusion that it is just as nerve-racking, just as exhausting, to go about with the two or three regulation suitcases as with ten or twelve. And when you arrive, the extra comforts those other eight or nine contain amply justify the excess baggage rates and all the fuss.

Originally I allowed myself to be conditioned by the idea that it was a nuisance to other people, as well as myself, if I had too much luggage. But now I know it's worth it, for me, and *tant pis* for other people. (If nothing broadens the mind like travel, equally, nothing hardens the heart so fast either.) How I wish I could say, like Mr. and Mrs. Averell Harriman, that I always take along a few good pictures, 'a little travelling collection' like theirs, a Picasso of the Blue period, a Douanier Rousseau, a Gauguin, and a Guardi or two. . . .

Always Travel Heavy

This question of a movable *cadre*, or transportable personal atmosphere must have been well understood by the Chinese, who by inclination travel with their entire home around them, and who specialized in all sorts of complicated yet simple pieces of furniture which hinged and could be taken to pieces to travel flat; delicate sheets of painted papier-maché which unfold into hanging cupboards, little tables, or wall brackets. I have several such pieces, once designed as part of a Chinese merchant's caravan, winding across Asia, week by week and halting, night by night, to be set up, a little Pekin in the Gobi desert, achieving this very personal *setting* to which I aspire more clumsily today.

In Europe, in the spacious days of the Grand Tour, that magic phrase which set the seal of aristocratic polish on the young gentleman who always voyaged through France and Switzerland to Italy and back, there was no nonsense about travelling light. Then, the great lumbering equipages were made to transport an entire way of life, and as they went lurching up over the St. Gothard Pass, the decanters of port shifted uneasily in their baize-lined mahogany inlaid boxes, the chased silver toilette sets jangled and the copper *batteries de cuisine* clinked; the postilions cracked their whips, the French tutor dutifully extolled the Alpine sunset and the young milord, lolling on the velvet, double-sprung upholstery, thought regretfully of cock-fighting, and yawned his way into Italy.

It must be admitted other ages have not travelled light. I recall the tragi-comic accounts of the retreat from Sedan, where the over-choked roads were further congested by the Emperor's chefs and hairdressers and their cumbersome equipment. Lord Byron travelled about with seven servants and an exotic menagerie, some pets, some designed for the table. One Russian nobleman took his private theatre with him when he travelled and beguiled the endless icy versts with performances of Molière and Hayden. Other Slavs of substance were installed in sable-lined coaches mounted on sledges, cumbersome as houses, often with a cow or two, to milk en route, and an orchestra of serfs, fiddling and scraping through the long dark nights. And we all know the legend of Catherine the Great's journey throughout her realm, not only surrounded by baggage coaches and escorts of Cossacks and various *soupirants*, but confronted, all along the route, by whole cardboard villages, hurriedly thrown up, an hour or two before her passage, to ensure an air of prosperity and population. That was travelling heavy in the grand manner.

Lady Blessington's departure for Italy, with her husband, and Count d'Orsay was the sensation of Paris in 1827. It was rightly called the Blessington Circus. They had endless baggage wagons and a retinue of servants, as well as a chef and his assistant, with all the egg-whisks, soufflé moulds and pastry-boards necessary to ensure the same Lucullus-like standards the trio had enjoyed at home. Lady Blessington's own carriage, designed by her doting husband, contained, among other things, a small but choice library, a writing-table, bedding, and a *chaise-longue*. . . . . Only forty years earlier, another sybaritic woman's insistence on travelling luxuriously (and heavily) had perhaps caused the death of herself and her family. When the Queen Marie-Antoinette was a prisoner in the Tuileries in 1791, her adorer, Count Fersen, planned her escape and would probably have achieved it, in spite of post-master Drouet's dash to call the Republican troops, if the Queen had not insisted on so many fabulous and Royal comforts that Fersen had to set about having a special carriage made, a *berline*, 'a stupendous new Coach', Carlyle calls it, which delayed the escape by weeks and proved to be both a noticeable and cumbersome affair, the last thing in which to make a dash over the frontier. Perhaps the ill-fated Queen remembered that luxurious *berline* when she was jolting her way to the scaffold in a tumbril.

My own excess baggage usually includes, besides a few picture books—*éditions d'art*, a favourite ikon, a Sheffield plate tea-pot (less fragile than china), and a pair of vermeil candlesticks found in a Saharan oasis, probably left there by some stylish French officer in the campaigns against Abd-el-Kader. Then, a toile de Jouey quilt embellishes any bed, and a rug—gros-point, not the travel kind of course—adorns all floors. I cram these objects, along with a radio, some small cushions and lesser comforts such as corkscrews, string and a magnifying glass into a wicker hamper, in itself decorative, unlike most luggage.

I should like to take a great many of the plants I collect wherever I go, for they, more than anything else, are companionable and beautiful, imparting an atmosphere of repose to even an overnight stop. But after I had tried to cram various examples of trailing and exotic vegetation into my suitcases, and had been told that there were quarantine regulations for plants as well as pets, and later discovered that many a cactus languishes on Ellis Island, I gave up the idea of a travelling greenhouse. But I did contrive to bring back a little pine tree from the Siberian taïga, coddling it all across the steppes of Central Asia, until it reached my roof-top terrace in Paris where it now thrives.

In spite of my insistence on creature comforts, and personal possessions, I do not bother overmuch about insecticides or bedding, things which are a 'must' with many far less demanding travellers whom I have sometimes seen instructing the Wagons-Lits attendant how to make up the bunk with their own monogrammed, crêpe-de-chine sheets, generously peppered with disinfectant. But then, by the time I have arranged myself in the middle of all my décor, I am so exhausted I can sleep anywhere. To travel heavy is to sleep heavy, too.

7

Every Picture Tells a Story

'Send us a card' is the classic, the inevitable farewell cry as the train pulls out of the station. As classic, as inevitable, the messages which come winging back from all manner of places: 'having a wonderful time', 'wish you were here'. For half a century, across a thousand different views the same phrases persist. Across the Sphinx, the Roman catacombs, (wish you were here...?), across the beach at Coney Island, Picasso's Harlequin or the Blue Danube. The range is vast. Jolly, geographic, historic, pornographic or artistic. Waggish, what the butler saw at Brighton; romantic, Rudolph Valentino savaging Vilma Banky; jokes about plumbing. The matriarchal Queen Victoria, embedded in a living wall of respectful relatives, half the *Almanach de Gotha*; so many of them, it is seen in retrospect, to lose, if not their heads, at any rate their crowns.

These old postcards, so glossy and reassuring, to Mum and Dad, Tiny or *Mon Vieux* are now strewn across the world, impersonal finds for collectors or just so much paper salvage. Lately, in France, their collection has become a new cult, rapidly assuming the intricacies and enthusiasms of stamp collection. Collectors are forming into clubs and subdivide their cards into sharply defined types. Out-of-the-way places are much sought after. So are exotic scenes, curious types or outstanding personalities. Some collectors go, too, for the stamp, which seems greedy. When all three combine, as for example, a card of Unter den Linden, bearing Russian army franking and Mr. Churchill's signature, it makes a really royal flush, a true collector's piece.

Some enthusiasts prefer cards of one specific sort, concentrating on one country or city alone; or railway engines, dogs, cathedrals, Geisha girls. Others go for the writing matter. Many dull cards are redeemed by the subject matter of their message. I have one which shows a group of ample Parsee ladies lolling together, gracefully draped in saris. It is addressed to a gentleman living in Manchester. 'Assassin!' is the unsigned message, brief and to the point. All sorts of speculations arise. . . . Another, perhaps my favourite, shows the Wailing Wall at Jerusalem, wailers in full cry. Across the corner we read, 'Kindest thoughts from Nettie and Papa.' One wonders why kindest thoughts . . . what were Nettie and Papa doing beside the Wailing Wall that August day in 1907? Delicious vistas open before us as we abandon ourselves to nostalgic fancies. . . . I shuffle my cards; here is the *bon-bon* prettiness of Gaby Deslys ('having a wonderful time' should have been her motto, or device). 'The Burning Ghats on the Ganges' calls for one or other of the classic postcard phrases. What range! A Mexican bullring picked out in sequins. The Alps. Piccadilly Circus on Mafeking night. 'The Scene of the Massacre Tea-Rooms', Glencoe.

The chief fascination of old postcards is their nostalgic quality. They show us a microcosm of some once ordinary way of life, now become extraordinary by its mere distance from our times. Through these cards we glimpse the humours and interests of another age. We see the charmers they chased, the jokes they enjoyed, and the events and objects they thought outstanding. I treasure an impressive scene of public vaccination at a town hall during an epidemic of smallpox in 1900.

Postcards are better for being mature. Their vintage years are at the turn of the century; their beginnings around the eighteen-seventies. Not much earlier. They are the first flowering of commonplace photography. After the great pioneer days of Daguerre and Octavia Hill came a vulgarized version of the medium that was accessible to all. Postcards record, for all times, aspects of the world which have now assumed legendary qualities. Some cards, as for example the coronation of the last Tzar, have become historic records.

Then, too, old postcards are doubly evocative, for they remind us not only of the places we have visited but, if they are really out of date, they probably conjure up the lost magic of those places which we always imagined romantically, in a way which, alas, the reality so often betrayed. They show us places which we have known, and also those we shall now never know. Places that have become inaccessible or changed beyond recognition. Pekin, the Great Within.... Names which haunt our imagination. Queen Tamara's castle in Georgia was such; but if I could go there now, should I find it as Lermontov knew it? Or should I reach it, earn it, perhaps, as a bonus for triple output—only to find it transposed into a shock-workers' rest home? Never mind, my brightly coloured card of the savage gorges and eagle-nest castle, with some superb Georgian cavaliers in the foreground, is all either I or Queen Tamara could wish.

The Sublime Porte, the Street of the Necromancers in Prague, the Kremlin, were other fabulous-sounding places of which I always dreamed. When at last I saw them with my own eyes I felt cheated. I took a bus to the Kremlin; I sighted factories beyond the Sublime Porte ... vistas of disillusion. It was not until, much later, looking through my cards (which are invariably found elsewhere, old Turkey in Edinburgh, or the Klondyke in Tunis) that I was able to recapture my original enchantment. This was the world as I had imagined it, and only through these cards could I now glimpse Proust's Paris or Dostoievsky's Russia.

Like the interests, the popular personalities of other days are incomprehensible to a later generation. The decline in sales of film or stage-star postcards can most likely be accounted for by the power of the cinema close-up and the number of magazines which provide suitable pin-up pictures. Thanks to the close-up, fans of today have the illusion of being far nearer to their adored than an earlier generation pining between long-range opera-glass peeps at matinée idols. It is curious to recall that in the late nineties, postcard personalities included, along with showgirls, a large number of religious leaders. The more handsome prelates are seen in full canonicals thundering from their pulpits. At the time of the Abdication, I cannot help feeling that some enterprising firm must have launched twin portrait cards of Mr. Baldwin and the Archbishop of Canterbury as pendant to those of the Duke of Windsor and Mrs. Simpson. But I have never seen one.

Politics have a place among picture postcards, but it is a small one. A card which I found, appropriately in Leningrad, of the baby Lenin, in a sort of Slavicized Fauntleroy suit, bubbling over with blonde curls and nestling into a plush armchair, is sometimes regarded as a political manifestation by my more literal visitors. I have seen extracts from Lenin's Order of Battle for the October Revolution made into the same sort of card as Mr. Churchill's, 'We shall fight on the beaches' . . . or the Atlantic Charter, which I saw embossed in Tudor-type lettering. But by and large, politics do not translate happily in postcard terms.

Although we do not, at first glance, associate the postcard with high moral purpose, yet this is sometimes its function. There are cards which list the Seven Deadly Sins, the Ten Commandments, or a Tract for the Times. Temperance societies avail themselves of this paper pulpit, but the only example I have is one publicized by the *Ligue Nationale contre l'Alcoolisme*, where the very title seems an anachronism in the language of a wine-drinking country.

European watering-places nearly always proffer, among the views of the Casino, *Jardin Botanique*, and *Plage*, a card of forbidding ugliness: this is certain to be described as *Le Temple Anglais*. All that perpendicular suburban architecture can do to render it repulsive has been done. But there must have been a demand, for the supply is everywhere apparent. I have a splendid example of this kind: it is addressed to a Mrs. Gilbert—at a London address. The message reads, 'Wish you were here. Your Gilbert'. More idle speculations: I see Gilbert embroiled in a delicious adventure, dividing his time between some unknown seductress and the gambling tables. I see it all. Emerging from the Casino a crumpled bankrupt wreck, now spurned by the lovely wanton from the Hotel Sumptuoso, he sees the pure dawn breaking and remembers his neglected little wife, his loved ones in London. Will he be forgiven? Not a moment to lose. He must write at once. He rushes to the station bookstall to buy a card. What card? Good God! Not that one—nor that one either. . . . Is there nothing suitable? Ha! *Le Temple Anglais!* The very thing. Seizing a pencil he writes his message 'Wish you were here. . . . The modest little postcard goes on its way, reassuring and homely; it will re-unite Gilbert and his loved one as no amount of telegrams could have done.

The different nationalities each have their specialities. English comics for great bawdy gusto, of which Donald Gill was the master, banana peel, lodgers, and smack-bottom fun. France for frisky stuff. Coy ladies being helped out of their corsets by sleek pink and white *poilus*. Elaborate charts of passion. *Thermomètres des amoureux*, where by an ingenious device a real blob of quicksilver mounts the card, according to the warmth of the hand (the force of passion, it is inferred). Entranced, we watch it soar from one illustrated stage of emotion to the next. From *amour timide*, by way of *amour passioné* to *folie amoureuse*, depicted as an engrossed couple in pastel underwear. There are pseudo-botanic cards, too, the language of flowers, with special emphasis on the message of the fig-leaf.

Germany and Roumania once excelled at 'feelthy' postcards, where the most frantic antics are displayed with a total lack of aesthetic or dramatic subtlety, and the singularly unattractive nature of most of the participants is as surprising as the frequent appearances of such extraneous objects as pince-nez and socks.

A rather adolescent form of humour which I much enjoy is to buy with an eye on some specific person, or occasion. Or I may hoard a card for years, till just the right moment arrives. For example, a highly coloured picture of the Etablissement Thermal, at Vichy, is obviously just the thing for corresponding with someone whose conduct in Occupied France was not altogether impeccable. And that detailed photograph of a head-on engine crash outside Perth, all mangled splintered scrap iron: that will be perfect to use as a week-end invitation card, listing Friday's best trains.

Many postcards remain teasing puzzles. That smudge beside the fountain, is it an Arabian charger or an ice-cream cart? Is this Europe, or Africa, or South America? Palms and volcanoes are singularly international when presented without a foreground. I peer into the tiny stage for further clues. 'Stands the church clock at ten to three?' and is there honey or hashish for tea in that lunar landscape? Yes: when all is said and done it is this mysterious quality which is the abiding delight of old postcards. Places we shall never see, people we shall never know. Places, faces, messages. A whole life's drama in a line of faded ink. A vanished epoch on an oblong of pasteboard.

8

The Time and the Place

Cities, like people, have their hour. This is their moment in time—their supremely personal expression of being, crystallized into an epoch which represents their essence and is the apotheosis of their spirit. Thus we can map time and track the hour and the place through centuries and across the world. . . . *'Last week in Babylon, last night in Rome'* . . . for although all time has existed in all places there is a strange light and shade, or focus, which sharpens our vision of certain places, at certain times, concentrating on that one moment, to make it symbolic of its century and its surroundings. Although this focus must be an individual one, and although it is remarkable how many people's view of the hour and the place correspond; but the subject is still highly controversial, the perspectives purely personal.

To me, Munich and Vienna are both Biedermeier cities— only Biedermeier, peopled with a late crop of Romantics, wearing stove-pipe hats and bottle-green frock-coats, carrying umbrellas, and playing upon the flute, at once poetic and prudent. For me, there are no Hapsburg glories; no Munich *putsch*, only Hermann and his Dorothea, trysting beneath the evening star, repairing to neat domestic interiors, or wandering in the brooding, yet meticulous twilight of Richter or Friedrich.

And Venice: for all its merchants, its Bucintoro splendours, the florid, swirling ease of Tiepolo and Veronese, or Carpaccio's round-rumped young bloods, jostling their gondola craft in the rank canal—for all these, I think Venice only lives imperishably in the eighteenth century. Transfixed, Casanova is forever escaping from the Leads. Behind a Ridotto grille, the *cavaliere servante* is always staking his sequins for his mistress, a nun. Longhi and Guardi caught the moment, Galuppi set it to music, and Goldoni staged it at the Fenice. Behind the sinistry of the beaked mask the comedy continues eternally. This is Venice, for all time.

But what of another Venice, you may ask? The city had its greatest being in another earlier age. Yet never was a place so dedicated to one moment—the eighteenth century. Later, the fervours of George Sand and Alfred de Musset seem oddly out of key among such ghostly but quintessential cynicism. So does Garibaldi's heroism, the Brownings' felicity, and the passions of Duse and D'Annunzio. But Cagliostro is at home there.

Yet Florence, surely, can never be *dix-huitième?* It must be the Middle Ages flowering into the Renaissance, with Dante, Giotto and the Medici as part of the noble procession. Here, Alfieri and his Countess d'Albany glide through the Florentine landscape, which is always that of a Benozzo Gozzali fresco, like wraiths, casting no shadow on the abiding Florence.

What makes this sharp focus, this selectivity of vision settle upon one time and place? The Akasish records (by which means some people explain Miss Moberley and Miss Jourdain's famous encounter with Marie Antoinette at Versailles) are supposed to be a never-ending, ever-present series of past events which can be recaptured by those who are attuned. These records do not, I believe, confine themselves to events of an intense, or significant nature alone. All times past are recorded there, to be experienced, and re-experienced by the initiate few.

It is not a city's most noble, or historic moment which is its apotheosis, in this sense. That would be subject to too much variation, according to the beholder. For that way, while the prelate sees Rome as the arena of Christian martyrdom, the classical scholar sees it as the city of the Caesars; though to me, being neither, it is the ornate frame for Renaissance and baroque Papal splendours—still a secular rather than ecclesiastical city. That way, too, Leningrad, to the balletomane, is Petroushka's Petersburg, while to readers of the *Daily Worker* it remains an anchorage for the cruiser *Aurora*.

Take Constantinople for example: the climax of Turkish history was most likely reached during the reign of Sülyman the Magnificent. And to the painter Liotard, who, two hundred years later was rendering the decaying charms of the Ottoman Empire in his meticulous manner, it was probably that sumptuous epoch—that, or the earlier, dark, ikon-studded Byzantium, which was the city's supreme moment in time. But to me, yet another two hundred years on, Liotard's epoch seems as remote as Sülyman's, or Justinian's, and of all three, I personally find Liotard's the most abiding.

It is the moment when West has conquered East. There is an Arcadian air, a conscious, almost self-conscious *Turquerie;* It is the setting for an endless *fête-galante,* centred round the crumbling Porte Sublime, where, in a summer sunset, a veiled houri is wooed with sherbet and sugar plums, and the voluptuous ghazels of the poet Nedim, and there is no menace of the Janissaries.

Like all America, New York is still forming. The fabulous city has not had time to distil itself into a past, let alone a perpetual moment, unless it proves to be the Frankie and Johnnie era, brash saloons and eager people.

Still mapping the centuries, while Leningrad has, for me, only one abiding moment—St. Petersburg, in the grandeur of its early nineteenth-century classicism—its Dekabrist and Pushkinian zenith—Moscow has two periods of perpetuity. It is still the mediaeval Asiatic village, a huddle of cruelty and colour which centres round the onion domes of Vassilli Blagennoie, and it is still the city of the rich merchants and wan gentry of the eighteen-fifties. The serfs are not yet liberated. The aristocrats fawn round the Winter Palace, seven hundred miles west, in St. Petersburg. But priest-ridden, greedy, fatalistic Moscow sits round its samovar spooning cherry jam from a saucer, sipping tea noisily, above the clang of a thousand belfries. This, for me, is forever Moscow: the burning of the Kremlin, the genius of Tolstoy and Dostoievsky —like the Streletzi Revolt or that of the Old Believers—are all manifestations of the Slav spirit, of Moscow's Asiatic vigour; so, too, is that curiously static force which Lenin was later to galvanize into one sweeping, dynamic and constructive whole, and which crystallizes in the Red Square. Yet for all its limitless impact, this is not Moscow's most essential aspect. Perhaps this is yet to come, if there is world enough, and time.

London, for all its past grandeurs, its quickened tempo obtained by the war years, and the influx of many races, does not find its moment in time either in its Tudor heyday, nor in the heroism of the bombardment. I find London was most perfectly itself only in the nineteenth century, when, with Regency Corinthians in curricles, tapping the claret and milling the Charlies, the city gathered momentum, and moving heavily but surely on, through vistas of materialism, it reached that unequalled expression of national form found in Cruikshank's London of the 'fifties.

This was the London of fogs and muffin-men: Hoxton pantomimes, gin palaces, meek governesses, great statesmen and mean streets. Public hangings. Landseer's lap-dog sentimentalities. A tight-laced, strait-laced hour that was, nevertheless, robust tough and kindly. It was the essence of the city, the century and the nation.

But Paris confounds all theories and eludes all dictums. Paris has the surface charm and flexibility of the true courtesan. Because of this, perhaps, it has contrived, for eight centuries, to be regarded as the essence of civilization by each succeeding age. '*Paris? Tu es le coeur du monde*', cried those most immobile of all Parisians, the Goncourt brothers, seeking no other world. There was a street for every century or mood. It was once for cynics and sentimentalists alike. Paris was the first night of Hernani blazing romanticism as a new creed; Voltaire's cynicism, Ravaillac's fanaticism and Dior's taste. The saccharinity of the *cartes postales*, and the noble logic of the Code Napoléon. Maxims, and the bistro round the corner. Existentialism and Cora Pearl, 'B.B.' and General de Gaulle stalking up the aisle of a delivered Notre Dame. But lately?

I wonder, does Paris now reflect, or create, claim, or repudiate? Is its present Americanization, *les blue-jeans*, and *le drug-store* on the Champs-Elysées something ephemeral, a teenager's dream, or one aspect of this age which Paris has truly absorbed? Perhaps Paris is the exception which proves my rule, that by charting the centuries we can find the setting for each moment in time. Call it the geography of time.

9

Much Holy Day

His dirty panama hat was studded with rubies and emeralds, or what passed for such in the Guatemalan highlands. He clambered up into the driver's seat of the bus. He was about four feet high, and his bare, prehensile toes clamped on to the clutch with simian agility. 'Good morning sir and lady,' he said courteously, 'my name is Tomàs. My father was a witch.'

'No, really?' we heard ourselves reply, in tinny social tones.

'He died in hell-fire', said Tomàs. 'Much sadness. I take you see his grave. Secret temple....' He eyed us roguishly. 'Many visitors not see ... but for you....'

As the overcrowded bus ground and shuddered its way up the mountain roads beside Lake Atitlàn he maintained a conversational flow, till we became close friends, bound together by ties of mutual interest and suffering. The sun smacked down; dust engulfed us, acrid and choking. Our parched mouths gaped, filling with grit and insects. Baggage flung itself off the rack at every hairpin bend. The cork blew out of a bottle of stomach-mixture, the elixir of life in these parts. Indeed, all journeys through Central America might be described as *Voyages aux Pays du Parégorique*. Although, except in jungle country, one is seldom very far from the pharmaceutical periphery, it is customary to travel with a basic pharmacy. Customary, and necessary.

We headed inland: there was a last glimpse of the volcano, San Pedro, reflected, still and majestic in the pellucid depths below Solalà. A signpost said: Huehuetenango via Sacapulas y Quiché.... It reads like the purest escapism. The bus plunged berserk into heavily wooded country, live oak, pine, and unnamable tangles, where lean pigs thatched with auburn curls rooted angrily. We were heading for Chichicastenango of mysterious legend.

'You been Mexico? Chichicastenango best,' said Tomàs with finality. It was, he continued, market day there. 'And tomorrow, very much Holy Day. Many blessings. You wait see', he beamed and squirmed, as he negotiated a particularly dizzy bend in the ravine road.

We now began to overtake groups of Indians struggling along, bent double under towering loads of merchandise reefed to their heads by a tump-line. Everything is carried this way: it is a habit begun so young that the typical back-slanting conical skull is said to be the result. Each *cargador*, as these carriers are called, is loaded with upwards of 200 pounds at a time, and rather than make an easy return trip unencumbered, they usually load up their packs with stones, to keep in training. They trotted fast, with tiny rapid steps, like little ponies. As they trotted, they chattered in high-pitched Chinese-sounding tones, and peeped at us from under their beetling loads with bright slit eyes. The other occupants of our bus now showed unmistakable pleasure. Their granite Mayan faces flickered into life at last. Superiority, pride, achievement ... it was all there. *They* were riding.

As we drove between narrow, windowless, white adobe-walled lanes, Tomàs accelerated furiously, and swinging round a blind corner on two wheels, came to a stop by backing into a market stall full of pineapples. Amid shrieks and imprecations, he leant out, took careful aim, and shot forward into a basket-stall kept by an angry man who spat at him. 'My enemy,' said Tomàs; 'tomorrow I pray for Mercy.' Bowing to us, he moved away from the stall-holders' spittle and fists, and was soon lost in the crowd.

We advanced among the mounds of merchandise, buying juicy local fruits, granadillos and cherimoyas, striped tiger masks and papier-maché jaguar heads, spotted pink and green, irresistible in their comic innocence. These are designed to be worn during the strange dances, rain invocations for the most part, which are still performed regularly hereabouts.

At Chichicastenango the whole elusive Guatemalan scene crystallizes. It is the hidden heart of Mayan country, with its own climate of mystical worship, of pagan rites and Papal rituals. The Quiché Indians' gods are inextricably interwoven. God the Father, God the Son, Great Lord of Retalevleu, the Prince of the Thunderbolts, Holy Mary, St. Peter and the Lordly Spirits who attend the Dawn. The Indians are as superstitious as pious. Nothing must be left to chance. After luxuriating in High Mass, at the church of San Tomàs, they hurry up into the hills to placate their stone idols with some suitable sacrifice. Some years ago, when all priests were proscribed, the Indians continued to come to church, punctiliously; but soon Rome was blended with pagan incantation. Today, the devout Indian goes to church accompanied by his own special witch-doctor; together they make the rounds of the chapels, strewing flowers, different coloured petals, according to their prayers, yellow for crops, white for health, pink for riches, or such. The witch-doctor is their mouth-piece, he frames their prayers and directs them where to place their candles. Together, client and priest inch up the great curve of stone steps on their knees, burning copal incense to their several gods.

Most Holy Day or not, Chichicastenango always wears a devotional air. All day, every day, it swims in a mauve haze of incense, curling in perfumed wisps round the brazier, which glows ceaselessly, outside the church door. Here the pilgrims and witch-doctors light their censers. Day and night the pious shuffle up the steps, blood seeping through the knees of their rough cotton trousers. But they do not seem to feel pain: their faces are rapt, ecstatic. There is much to pray for: little has been given, here, besides beauty.

Much Holy Day

At the inn they told us to be up and out early if we wanted to see the processions, and after a night punctuated by explosions, which we later learned were fire-crackers let off to propitiate jealous local gods, we were on the main square as the sun topped the far hills and gilded the great bell clanging overhead. Already the village was filling up with streams of Indians and their wives and children gathering from all over the countryside. Each village wore its own distinctive costume. Men from Solalà in pink and white striped, calf-length trousers and tiny Eton jackets embroidered across the back in what looked like a huge, rather sinister butterfly, but which is said to be a version of the double-headed Habsburg eagle of the Spanish monarch Carlos V. Women from across the lake at San Antonio in their tight, scarlet ankle-length hobble skirts, their goitre-puffed throats hung with as many as thirty gold and silver blown-glass bead necklaces. The Quiché Indians, in virtue of their aristocracy, wore a sixteenth-century costume deriving straight from the Conquistadores, black doublet and hose, their heads bound pirate-wise with a red cotton handkerchief. The proudest families wore extra gold embroideries, blazing suns and moons, and were hung with gold chains of office.

They were all forming into processions now. Each group carrying, or rallying round, a life-sized saint's statue which had been removed from its chapel to be paraded through Chichicastenango three times before being restored to its place.

Many of these saints are home-made versions of the original Spanish statue; lovingly re-created Indian versions of the baroque original. They were button-eyed, scarlet-cheeked, jolly figures, hilarious martyrs, at once touching and grotesque. They looked like gigantic toys designed by Steinberg. Some woolly bearded saints carried an infant (but also bearded) Christ-child. They were dressed in brilliant artificial satins, often mixed with fabulous laces, cotton ankle-socks peeping from beneath their fine robes, peacock feathers (symbol of the Cotinga bird, whose turquoise plumage once adorned Montezuma's mantle of kingship), and loops of stiff gold bullion fringe or scraps of cheap ribbon safety-pinned on to them in a haphazard manner. Overhead were arbours of spruce branches hung with little bells and winking pocket shaving mirrors from the five and ten-cent store.

These extraordinary carnival figures swayed and tottered as they were slowly paraded. Before and after them, paced the Quiché nobles, bearing tall staves of office, each topped by a blazing silver-gilt sun. Their grave faces remained unmoved, even when the more uncontrollably devout followers let off fireworks round them, soaring rockets and Catherine wheels, gunpowder play in the manner of an Arab fantasia.

Inside the church, the organ wheezed out a tremolo of Monteverdi from behind the ornate screen. The procession moved towards the high altar, where an old priest waited for them with a smile of welcome. The women, bunched up with shawls and babies, squat, squaw-like figures, followed their men at a respectful distance. Even before God, their place is the lowliest.

At the moment of the Elevation of the Host, the hush was shattered by the roar of rockets, ripping the silence from outside, where some of the witch-doctors were acting as a sort of extra-mural congregation: translating the holy ritual into more generally appreciated terms of gunpowder, sulphur and brimstone. Presently, as the church emptied, trotting lines of Indians head for the hills, making for more ceremonies, while others settled to an afternoon's bargaining, among the stalls full of cotton handkerchiefs, serapes, nameless bits of meat and entrails, coarse household china or *tequila* booths.

Tomàs, who had followed us into the church and pestered us continually to provide him with a sum suitable to both the offertory and his devout nature, now skipped around us as we moved from stall to stall.

'My father invite you to his home now,' he said. 'Very holy party, much interesting prayer and dance.'

'But I thought you said he was dead?'

'Risen again,' said Tomàs triumphantly. 'My father a Christian witch. . . .'

Eyeing him sternly we said we were busy and shook him off.

As the day wore away and the stalls were packed up, the sound of shooting merged with the rockets; but no one, at first, realized violence was afoot. Presently a terrible wailing sounded. *'Crime passionnel'*, said the chemist's assistant, who had spent a year in Geneva, and spoke basic French. A woman rushed out of one house and into another: we saw a heavy, sleepy-looking gendarme waddle across the square, buttoning up his white uniform as he went. There had been trouble between two brothers, we were told. One was dead; the other was dying. . . .

Tomàs made a jack-in-the-box appearance at our side.

'You want see body?' he asked hopefully.

'Do go away!' we said.

He went off, looking offended.

The last stalls were dismantled; the *tequila* booths emptied, and the more incapacitated drinkers lay where they fell, giving the empty market place the appearance of a battlefield. Tomàs was now among the fallen, his jewel-studded panama hat crushed in the dust. He was snoring gently.

'So much for his very holy day,' Romain said, and stepped carefully over him. We did not wish for further solicitations.

The sun dropped suddenly. All at once it was cold: twilight raced over the countryside, and the incense braziers glowed from the church steps. The evening star hung low over the jacaranda trees, as some indignant women began to search among the log-like figures on the ground. As each one found her man, she dragged him up, and went off, scolding and supporting the inert bundle.

That night, nested-down in the enclosed, secret world of

comfort and plumbing provided by the Mayan Inn, we watched a marimba band stump on to the patio and settle to their enormous, unwieldly white-wood instruments. They began to play spanking local airs; the macaws shuffled round on their perches, their gaudy plumage lit by the firelight flickering out from the kitchens. They eyed the musicians balefully, and began to outshriek them.

In our room a log fire roared up the tiled stove. Far away across the mountains, rockets still soared and sparked; and fire-crackers still exploded in night-long rites designed to placate the Gods of Harvest and Rain, and the Lord of the Morning. As if in reproof, the church bell clanged out, suddenly restless. A thin wraith of incense drifted across the darkness outside our window and hung there, like a pale pall. Far away, a dog barked and was answered by another. Chichicastenango slept. It had been, as Tomàs said, a much holy day.

But perhaps, after all, not so very much holy: before midnight the midget reprobate had recovered sufficiently to come scratching on our shutters.

'You want see bad ladies interesting dance?' he whispered.

'Not tonight,' we replied . . . 'tomorrow, maybe. . . .'

'Tomorrow no good: not holy day', he replied, unctuously, and giving us no time to change our minds, he disappeared into the night.

10

Many Mexicos

The theatrical aspect of Mexican daily life is overpowering: the fierce light beats down, an assault, and the shadows cast by the paeons' huge-brimmed sombreros give their faces a skull-like relief, black eye-sockets and sunken, fleshless jaws, recalling the apocalyptic wood-cuts of Posada, the Daumier of Mexico. Every scene is both convulsive and dramatic. In the shadow of the sumptuously gilded church, a landslide of garbage glows brilliant with rotting fruit and offal. Lean dogs prowl, men fight with knives, and a graceful creature, delicately boned as an Aztec princess, draws her *reboso* about her head— a street Madonna, nursing her child, unmoved.

So many layers of civilization and savagery here: Aztec, Toltec, Zapotec, Mayan, Spanish, French, American. . . . Maximilian as well as Montezuma. The terrible sacrificial pyramids of Teotihuacan can be seen from the terrace heights of Maximilian's palace at Chapultepec, where Montezuma's giant ahuehuete trees still shade the park. And down in the city, neon lights play across the blistering baroque of a church where Cortez' priests said Mass. Vistas and *aspectos* everywhere.

JUCHITÀN

Across the cactus-studded hills, a cloud of dust resolves into a group of horsemen: bold, centaur figures, galloping into town, bent on mischief, by their looks. They rein up abruptly, beside an ambulant photographer's booth, and kneeling before a primitive painted back-cloth depicting the Miraculous Virgin of Guadalupe, they strike attitudes of theatrical piety, hands clasped, liquid black eyes rolled heavenwards, as if perceiving some ecstatic vision, and are so recorded for their loved-ones, and posterity. Yet, watching them, we shiver: they are cruelty incarnate. It is their Aztec heritage. The sacrificial pyramids of the past are more real, to them, than the archaeologists' Mecca they have now become. The next bend in the road may well reveal that terrible execution scene of Eiseinstein's *Thunder Over Mexico*, victims buried up to their necks, their heads ridden down by yelling horsemen.

MEXICO CITY

Prison, like death, is not generally feared, however much, to the stranger's eye, conditions appear those of an engraving by Gustav Doré. Until lately, prisoners carried, and perhaps still carry, arms, a gun or a knife, as protection against other prisoners. Children are with their mothers, and a new women's prison is now being completed, where conditions will be very progressive, with crèches and gardens. In many prisons and particularly the penal settlements near Vera Cruz, whole families move in with the criminal, sharing his cell and sentence.

At the Central Prison of Mexico City, an enlightened rule admits the flesh, in the person of prisoners' wives and sweethearts on weekly visits, many hours at a time, behind closed cell doors. The huge noisy crowd of women surges forward through the gates, shrieking like parakeets, gaudy skirts swirling, teeth flashing. Their men are waiting for them, shouting and stamping. One by one the cell doors clang shut on their joys. It is quiet now. The guards lean against the courtyard walls lit by the sinking sun, picking their teeth, looking bored. In the simplicity of human relationships Mexican life recalls that of a more lusty Europe, when camp-followers and *vivandières* marched with the armies.

PEDIGRAL

Elegant, wealthy Mexicans create new standards of luxury living among the black lava fields of Pedigral, where glass and steel architecture seems an organic part of the landscape. There are no trees, no flowers here: only the geometric forms of the villas break the harshness. They are painted astonishingly, lemon or turquoise roofs, one wall salmon, another lilac. Flocks of white doves circle round them, reflecting the colours in an iridescent flash of wings, theatrically brilliant against the lava. When Madame Calderon de la Barca went to Mexico in 1840 as the young Scottish bride of the first Spanish envoy, she described 'the Pedigral' as being an immense formation of ferruginous lava and porphyritic rock, looking as if cursed for some crime committed there.

OAXACA

At dusk, the ilex trees glistened with the first lamp-light. Whole families of grey squirrels which had been chittering and frisking in the foliage now darted down to drink the dew from the ornamental flower-beds below. When they sipped, they shut their eyes, like wine connoisseurs. The markets were closing, and the cafés were opening. All along the street beside the fruit market, crouched a line of women and young girls, selling off the fruits and food which would not be saleable next day. Each huge basket contained, beside its now dubious wares, an oil lamp lighting the beautiful, stony faces from below, footlight-wise. They preened and ogled the passers-by, shouting bawdily, for they, too, were for sale, along with the melons, aguacates, chayotes, papayas and cherimoyas. Exotic fare.

SAN MIGUEL ALLENDE

Behind the convent, a line of *black* washing, nuns robes, flaps crow-like and incongruous in the sunlight.

CHOLULA

The sound of flute and marimba, and a soft, joyous song comes nearer. We stand under the orange trees and watch the procession. It is a baby's funeral. One man carries the shoe-box-sized cardboard coffin on his shoulder. The mourners follow, grave-faced, but not grieving. Life is hard; the baby has escaped; he is with God! They dance, a jigging step, and sing a sort of abstract, stylised expression of joy, in keeping with the Mexican's voluptuous pleasure in death. Hereabouts it is quite customary for a rich family to purchase the corpse from a poor household, thus acquiring a reason for holding an elaborate festival of death—a wake. This way, all are satisfied: the poor, that their dead has a splendid burial; the rich, that they have the occasion to celebrate death worthily.

SAN JOSÉ DE PURÙA

A luxury hotel is pitched down like an expensive toy, in wildest, richest, loveliest country. The yellow, radioactive pool drips with bougainvilia and roses. Waiters scuttle over from the main building with trays of sustenance. The parakeets shriek and flitter in the eucalyptus groves, and the tourists pile their belongings under the sun umbrellas, towels, scrabble sets, and small, unobtrusive crocodile jewel-cases. That way they can keep an eye on them. Bandit country! The bare hills quiver in the noonday blaze: rocky, remote, streaked with waterfalls, they are the perfect setting for a brigand's lair. The happy tourists plunge in, surfacing often, like hippos, keeping a wary eye trained on the jewel-cases, boiling away their ailments, their wrinkles, their overweight, their past. . . . And then, a Mexican Indian girl sways down the road, on bare, patrician feet, staring ahead, aloof and indestructibly beautiful in her bone structure, her womanly grace. The tourists watch her out of sight. A shadow seems to have fallen over their play.

'Homer! I guess we'll go into lunch now', says a rather fretful voice. . . . One by one, the towels, the scrabble boards, and the crocodile jewel-cases are collected, reassuring symbols of civilization. At luncheon, most of the visitors bring portable radios to their tables, to croon them through the courses. . . . No more need to talk, to think . . . no more loneliness or strangeness. The hearty tones of a 'commercial' rise above the clatter of crockery. No more sense of being far away. They are home.

SOUND AND FURY

There are gardenias floating in the yellow-tiled pool of our hotel courtyard, and the sheets and pillows are edged with a lovely coarse hand-made lace. But Mexicans need little sleep, it seems, for sounds of the most exuberant life are all round us. Romain complains of the uproar, if we leave the windows open; yet how to sleep in this heat, with them shut? Night life in Mexico City reaches its apogee with Mariachi bands and revellers, around dawn, just as the markets spring to life. Romain has scoured the place for ear-plugs, without success. Arriving at Taxco, in a room overlooking the little plaza, made golden by the sumptuous cathedral, and shaded by the profound, yet sparkling depths of the ilex trees, he is still confronted by the problem of noise, to which is now added the clanging and tolling of bells, almost overhead, and the clatter of mule-hooves. We eat in a particularly deafening bistro, but here, the pneumatic white bread gives Romain the idea it could be rolled into pellets as substitute ear-plugs. We set aside some more bread from the heart of the breakfast rolls, and for two nights it works perfectly. Then excruciating ear-ache sets in. Twenty-four hours later we have hired a taxi, and Romain greenish, like the evening sky, and in furious pain, is being rushed back to civilization. Every jolt in the road is agony. 'Not that I shall survive the local doctors anyhow', he says, almost with relish, for he is partial to disaster. I suggest that quite a large proportion of Mexicans appear to be treated satisfactorily in the splendid new hospitals, but he is unconvinced. 'And how will you make them understand my state? Remember, you speak no Spanish,' he continues, triumphantly, and now predicts that his brain will undoubtedly be affected if we do not reach help within the hour. The driver grunts, and accelerates with passion, speeding us through the blackness of the Mexican night. Romain is now giving me last-minute instructions for his funeral—by cremation—and advises me how to conduct my widowhood. It is a harrowing journey.

At the hotel I ask for an English-speaking doctor, and almost at once, he telephones.

'What seems to be the matter, Señora?'

'Well, doctor, it's like this, my husband has been stuffing breakfast rolls into his ears for the last four days, and now. . . .'

'Would you mind repeating that, Señora?'

I repeat this unusual piece of information.

'Then I think I'd better come round immediately,' he replies, and soon after appears, radiating skill and confidence. The information that he was trained at the celebrated Mayo Clinic in Rochester, Minnesota, comes as quite an anticlimax.

SOUTHWARDS

Leaving Mexico City before dawn, to fly down to the Chiapas Indian country, we saw many paeons still sprawled in the booths and *tequila* bars behind the Thieves Market. Acetylene flares sharpened the scene dramatically. Noisy Mariachi bands were still playing: the more prosperous paeons were munching some unplaceable meal—supper, breakfast? It was a dark mess, chocolate and pimento and entrails, oozing from between the eternal tortillas.

Flying southwards, we watched the sky lighten; it burned an electric green; suddenly the sun rose over great Ixctaccihuatl.

Our flight followed its snowy flank, over the crumpled brown canyons, on southwards, where nothing lived, and where every conical hill was an extinct volcano. Sometimes we traced a thread of track across the desolation, but there were no roads.

'Mont Alban!' shouted the pilot, and dipped the little plane sharply, swooping low over the vast Zapotec courts and pyramids lying below us, geometric and grim. Even in our plane (safe in our plane, we felt, by comparison with the legends of human sacrifice and Aztec cruelties) we seemed to hear the ascending shrieks of the victims as their beating hearts were torn from them by the priests' black obsidian knives.

In the Chiapas country of south-east Mexico, towards the Guatemalan border all is changed. No more exoticism—the tropics give place to Switzerland, pine forests, a chilly, misty upland, inhabited by what appear to be Tibetan monks. The Chamulas look strongly Asiatic, flat yellow faces, Mongol eyes, and a shaggy thatch of hair like black fur—no sleek plumage here. They are gravely civil, but watchful, and unenthusiastic towards strangers. They see very few, for their villages lie high in the hills, reached, if at all, by rocky tracks. They are greatly occupied with their own special pagan rituals and medicine.

The traditional Mexican passion for, and belief in, strange drugs, secret spells and herbal concoctions, malefic or curative, continues unabated: but here, besides the necromancers' booths at country markets, where love-philtres and darkly powerful powders guaranteed to bring about both births and deaths are sold, there is a purely contemporary aspect too: INJECIONES says a roughly printed card in many windows along the cobbled main street. This means that penicillin, hormones and multiple vitamins, as well as less specific kinds of local drugs, are freely obtainable, and as freely injected, by the local nurse, the inn-keeper, or the woman across the way. . . .

Among the Chamula Indians, modern medicine is a subject of absorbing interest. In the remote villages set high in the bare,

Thibetan-like uplands, they are properly proud of their medical centre. A small, well-equipped clinic is run by a doctor and nurse, whose base it is, between enormous mountain rounds. One or two especially gifted Chamula men, village leaders, were trained as assistants, to act in the doctor's absence. Alas! Having mastered the aseptic technique, their zeal became almost insensate: the limited supplies of rubber gloves, sterilized gauzes, hypodermic needles, surgeons' masks and all the panoply of the operating theatre had been expended on every head-cold, liver complaint or croupy brat brought in for advice. Now, save for real emergencies, a return to more casual curative methods is encouraged.

SAN CRISTOBAL LAS CASAS

A bleak, austere land; nothing tropic here. We watch the eagles soaring high above the black forests, where a band of Zinacothék Indians hunt them with crazy flint-lock guns dating from Iturbides's reign. Those Zinacothéks are the fops of Central America, their build, manner and costume mark them as a race apart. They appear to have stepped from some eighteenth-century 'Embarkation for Cythère', a canvas by Hubert Robert, all roses and cupidons, rather than the mountains and gorges that are their home. Their clothes are wildly improbable. The men wear a short—very short—tunic of pink and white striped linen, over long, bare legs and elegantly sandalled feet; the whole topped by little straw hats tipped coquettishly over one ear, and bunched with pale coloured satin ribbons, like a Watteau shepherdess; most of them carry guitars, also ribbon-trimmed, made from armadillo shells. Sometimes we came on groups of them sitting by the road, thrumming their guitars and singing, roadside troubadours. Their women are seldom seen, and remain as utilitarian and drab as any hen-bird. These peacock-fops look an idle, seducing lot. It was as if a troupe of strolling players, costumed for one play, had strayed by chance into the scenery of another: some *fête galante* by Marivaux in Pastor Manders' thunderous setting.

LOS POBRES AND PRIVILEGIADOS

Nights are penetratingly cold here. Some of the Indians arrive at the market place in San Cristobal de las Casas before dawn, having walked all night to get there. They watch for the rim of sun to appear over the mountains, *La Capa de los Pobres*—the poor man's mantle, they say, waiting patiently for its rays to warm them through.

But we, guiltily conscious of being *los privilegiados*—the rich ones, the tourists—order our breakfast coffee laced with *eau de vie* before plunging into another day of enraptured wandering.

TOWARDS TEHUANTEPEC

Zigzagging across the country we reach the Isthmus of Tehuantepec, on the Pacific. En route, we are stuck for twenty-four hours at some unpronounceable halt. The only restaurant is a street booth; the menu, *tequila*, or a cup of chocolate, and a local delicacy, reminiscent of potted shrimps, but made of some kind of small worm-like insect—fried. There is no bread other than the paw-paw or bread-fruit trees which grow exuberantly.

✤   ✤   ✤

At Tapachula, a brazen heat pours down like liquid fire. Above the town the coffee fincas quiver in the heat haze. Down below, in the town, it is clammy. All along the wildly cobbled streets, thatched shacks are topped by a line of huge brooding black birds—zapilotes, a kind of vulture. Tiny green parakeets, clowns of the bird world, perch on the heads of drowsy dogs, or ride, staggering and lurching, on the top of the towering laundry baskets which majestic matrons carry on their heads. Even at noon there is no siesta hush. The voices of women, children and macaws merge into one chattering shriek. The streets peter out into twining coiling jungles, where there are pumas, alligators . . .

✤   ✤   ✤

NIGHT-PIECE

At dusk, the population assemble round one of those tiny, ornate, white-painted iron bandstands that are found in every Mexican town. They are said to have been inaugurated by the Empress Carlotta and remain a symbol of her refining efforts. A marimba band, opulently dressed in white and gold naval uniforms, plays Strauss passionately. Their bare feet issue, with prehensile vigour, from below their richly braided trousers. At the end of each number they applaud each other warmly. Birds stir uneasily in the shining dark depths of the ilex trees. The elaborate street lamps, clusters of incandescent globes, light the lovers, sitting in respectable proximity—but no more. Their beautiful Zapotec faces are grave, aloof in sorrow, in pleasure, in love. The band packs up for the night. The crowd disperses in twos and threes, towards the outskirts, swamps, trailing swags of rubbery vegetation, nothingness.

We walk home through shuttered byways. Outside a last livid-lit *pulquéria*, or pulque-bar, the peons are sprawled asleep, their machetes beside them. We step over them gingerly. Back at the hotel, we arrive at an unfortunate moment. The night watchman has brought out his pet anaconda, an enormous, bolster-like snake, said to be harmless, but not prepossessing. It is a species much used in the Isthmus of Tehuantepec, as mouser and general household pet. 'He fine on rats,' says the watchman proudly. We hurry upstairs and slam our door.

✤   ✤   ✤

All night the Berlé-lé shrills its peculiar note, piercing, monotonous. Oddly, this too is regarded as a household pet. Everywhere, the sinister zopilotes—huge carrion birds—sit brooding on the roofs or fences, even along the rail of our balcony, a frieze of doom, that flaps down to scavenge in the gutters. 'Make healthy,' said the café waiter indulgently; and maybe they do, in this region of indifferent sanitation. But they are not engaging.

CHRISTMASTIME

This is our third visit to Mexico. We have fled the tinsel-hung boulevards of Hollywood, the lingerie-pink Father Christmases and the baby-blue reindeer which express the fantasy of Californians at this season; we will taste again the *âpre* grandeurs of Mexico. From a tinselled and starred airport we emerge into streets hung with grotesque straw figures, carnival puppets, and in every lighted shrine, rapt, baroque saints. Before the cathedral, the children are forming processions with lanterns and candles bobbing in the dusk. Some mothers carry babies in arms, their midget Murillo faces wondering, their pudgy fists grasping lighted candles, dangerous, but delightful.

Romain and I share Scrooge's detestation of the festive season: we fled its bonhomie in California, yet we find it even here. Along Juarez Avenue, the tourist gift shops are stacked with alligator luggage and silver-ware labelled (in English) FOR HIM—FOR HER. A straggle of paeons put down their bundles, and stare. The men have coarse striped serapes over their traditional white cotton clothes, and the women are huddled into their shawls, or *rebosas*, for it is surprisingly cold. The brilliant Christmas star hangs huge and low over the magnolia trees of the Alameda gardens, where a troop of mummers are posturing and prancing, keeping Christmas with strange pagan rituals. Christmas everywhere; even here, the hotels rustle with tissue paper wrappings, Christmas cards, and the inevitable commercial blackmail. Where can we escape it? Cuernavaca will be pullulating with tourists, and the rich polyglot residents will have abandoned themselves to turkey and tinsel. Pueblo? Talapa? Acapulco. . . . Oh! no, *not* Acapulco. It has become the Eden Roc of Central America. There will be Christmas dinner beside the swimming pools.

But Romain settles the question by deciding he will start writing a new book, a memoir of his youth. He sees just how it must go. Mexico can wait, so can dinner. No sooner unpacked than he has sent out for reams of paper, bottles of ink and several pens, a spectacular writer's outfit. He sits down with his back firmly to the window. Page 1, Chapter 1, and *La Promesse de l'Aube* is begun. I go out to dine on fiery foods alone, and return to find him on to page 27. This is the stuff. This is the way we see writers write in the theatre, or the films; as painters paint, or for that matter, people pack suitcases, concentrated action, no hesitations, no indecisions, as in real life.

POSTSCRIPT. Before our Christmas holiday was over the first draft was completed. Romain had given himself over totally into the dark grip of memory and seen nothing at all of the Mexico he loves. But he had escaped Christmas.

CHAPULTEPEC

The feathery pepper trees shade a terrace which overlooks the city far below. Here Carlotta and Maximilian paced, united by their failures as much as their ambitions. He, pouting over some point of Hapsburg protocol to be adapted to the Mexican court; she, planning where to plant another of those florid little wrought-iron band-stands she strewed about the furthest townlets of her wild domain. They still stand, frivolous monuments to a tragic empress; but when the people gather, solemn, in pleasure as in pain, to hear a marimba band whacking local airs or Gershwin, a breath of patchouli and an echo of Offenbach seems to fall on the scene, recalling that Second-Empire Paris which sponsored Maximilian's brief reign.

Proud, ineffectual Carlotta is most clearly seen at Chapultepec, for her private suite is still much as she left it: a series of bourgeois, overstuffed salons, dark, in spite of the brilliant Mexican sunlight outside. Carved ebony furniture, a fusty canopied bed; two rosewood grand pianos, where she and her husband sat back to back, galloping through duets by Meyerbeer, and an inlaid writing-desk where she scribbled away the fateful days.... Long-nosed, proud Carlotta, bent over the emblazoned sheets of paper, scribbling her interminable letters to the Empress Eugénie. It was Empress to Empress. 'Madame and good sister,' she wrote, 'we trust in God and are very content. My Mondays are really most successful . . . small gatherings of guests, fifty or so. . . .' And all the while, the implacable Indian faces were closing in. The fifty guests dwindled to the fourteen ladies in waiting . . . soon the Court ceased to exist. When the French troops were withdrawn and the last battle lost, only two men stood beside the Emperor, facing the firing squad on the Hill of the Bells, at Querétaro. Even the embalmers failed him. What remained of the Emperor had to be swathed in mummy-like bandages, from head to foot, before it could be returned in state to Vienna.

But as Carlotta had gone mad, some months earlier, when visiting the Vatican to plead her husband's cause, she was spared all knowledge of the final failure.

LAKE PASCUARO

I crept out of the house very early one morning. I like to watch a village wake. The women were fanning their charcoal braziers, beside the open door. Overhead, brilliant spangled birds flittered in the tall eucalyptus trees. The church bell clanged to the counterpoint of tortillas smacking on the stones, plip-plop, a flabby sound. Along the lake, a group of fishermen were mending their strange looped figure-of-eight nets: they looked like gigantic butterflies settled on the still surface of the water. It was a pastoral scene; a lyric landscape. But brigand-infested too. The men had scowling, blackly beautiful faces. Beside them lay their striped serapes and machetes: these last, murderously curved knives, are as much a symbol of Mexican daily life as the furled umbrella to London. One man, eyeing me stonily, picked up his machete, and licking his thumb, ran it along the blade. As I faltered, he bent forward with a sudden swoop—and began slicing at his toe-nails. He looked up under his huge straw hat: he was laughing, showing a double row of broad, perfect, primeval-looking teeth. But his eyes retained their basilisk stare. Whey-faced ladies should not prowl about alone—even in the morning, he seemed to say.

YUCATAN

Here, yet another aspect of Mexico is found—something quite apart, in spirit as in fact. Yucatan remains aloof, almost inaccessible. Ships must lie several miles out to sea, beyond the shallows. Only one track-like road runs through the brush: a plane flies in two or three times a week, stopping there between Mexico and U.S.A. Once Merida, the capital, was the centre of the world's sisal or hemp trade. Now the forgotten little city lives becalmed in its fabulous archaeological past. The lost splendours of the Mayan cities overpower its modest present. A green web of jungle spreads beyond the ruins of temples, plumed-serpent pyramids and past glories to encroach on the living city. At twilight, the sky turns a pale, bright mauve, and merges in a lilac haze with the deeper mauve of the jacaranda trees. In the cathedral, there is more mauve; the choristers wear parma-violet robes beneath their lace-trimmed tops. Later, we saw them in the main square. They were eating violet ices (*Elegantes y Delicadoes*), and having their pointed patent leather boots cleaned by even smaller, more simian-looking boys, while a sumptuous middle-aged lady with a lace parasol stood treat, from an open carriage drawn up beside the kerb. I wonder: did Ronald Firbank know Merida? He is recalled at every turn.

PALENQUE AND UXMAL

Eighty per cent of the local population is Mayan: among themselves Mayan is the current language. Their parrots, too, sound these incomprehensible syllables. Mayan standards of beauty once included bow-legs, receding foreheads achieved by bandages; and a squint, this being arrived at by strings fixed before the babies' line of vision. The present-day citizens, while comely, do not come up to the dazzling standards of the other Mexican provinces: from time to time the diabolic or grotesque masks of Mayan gods are still to be traced in the living Meridans.

CAMPECHÉ

Saturday night: the Salon de Bellezza (plugging a line of magenta nail varnish) works overtime preparing the local beauties for the ball tonight. Cantinflas, the Charlie Chaplin of Mexico, is billed at the movie-house. There is molé and baby shark on the menu at Pancho Pistoles restaurant. We will drive there in one of those strange little open carriages peculiar to Yucatan, with cracked, peeling leather curtain-flaps enclosing the passengers with a sort of harem secretiveness. They have an air of sinistry and intrigue, and seem at once ambulant confessional box and *maison de rendez-vous*. What dark drama lurks within? We imagine some Meridan Emma Bovary rattling to her doom in such an equipage.

PROGRESSO

A broken-down line of buses runs between Merida and Progresso, in the mangrove-swamp country along the mustard-yellow, brackish Gulf of Mexico. These buses have religious names. Ours was labelled Nostre Dama del Succoro. There were no springs, or glass in the windows either. Furnace heat, weighted by grit, blasted us as we bounced along through the cactus and sisal plantations; a peon sitting next to me had a parrot on his shoulder: like everyone hereabouts, it spoke Mayan: racy talk, I fancy, by the applause.

The journey was enlivened by several stops when everyone drank milk from fresh coconuts. Our driver hacked them open for us with his machete. A blind guitarist paid his passage in kind, and everybody requested their favourite tunes, which he obligingly rendered. The driver was after the little señorita in pink on the back seat, and kept asking for some song about a dove. What would the French señora like they asked me, bowing gallantly? My mind went blank. I could only think of Wagner.

FISH AND FOWL

In the blood-red waters of the mangrove swamps around Campeché, cormorants waddle intently after fish, hopping from one serpent-like root to the next. They are followed by pelicans, croaking like operatic frogs. Their grotesque beaks are used by the farmers for drilling holes in the ground, when sowing seeds.

HUMAN SACRIFICES

We arrive at Chichén Itzà in the blaze of noon—the whole scene quivers. We crawl towards the Astronomers' Palace, the Nunnery, the Warriors' Temple, the Ball Court—steps, steps, walls of steps. We climb, we scramble and climb again. Lost splendours loom over us, plumed serpents and diabolic masks, almost as Catherwood drew them, more than a century ago.

We follow an overgrown track, tick-infested and thorny, through the brush. It leads to the Sacred Well, a brackish pool lying about sixty feet below our path. A sinister silence hangs over the place. No bird sings. All Chichén Itzà is a monument to cruelty. Here some of the sacrificial victims were thrown to their doom. On this curved altar stone the priests disembowelled others. Down these steps which we climb so painfully they flung the still palpitating hearts of human sacrifices.

And are we not also, in one way, human sacrifices on the altar of culture? Romain and I are not really archaeologically inclined. We begin to flag.

Above us, towers the pyramid of El Castillo, constructed at an angle of sixty degrees, making the climb a vertiginous martyrdom. Since Catherwood's day the steps have been cleared of vegetation, and their nudity makes the descent more terrifying, for there is nothing to clutch at, or break one's fall. The Sanctuary of El Tigre, the red tiger, is at the summit of a perpendicular, inter-pyramidal ascent. Pouring with sweat we begin the airless climb, ever higher, till El Tigre is revealed, glowing crimson, studded with jade. How many ages has he lurked in these stone heights? Suppose the door should jam? Suppose a wall should crumble? The accumulated weight of centuries, masonry, and terror closes in.

Enough! We precipitate ourselves down, and out, into the green living world around us.

The perfume of the datura flowers mingles with the smell of bean stew issuing from the guardian's hut. We hear the familiar plip-plop sound of tortillas being patted into shape. No more pyramids! Not one more ruin!

Unrepentant, we will return to Merida, savouring the animation of the collective taxi. We will watch the sun slant behind the palms; we will gorge ourselves on aguacates and

chayotes and cherimoyas, fruits of paradise. . . . We will go to
the Salón de Billares El Olimpo, and watch *los correctos* (the
elegant Mexicans) playing chess under the ilex trees in the
plaza, while the marimba band is in full whack. Tomorrow we
will go and bathe in the opaque mustard-yellow Gulf of
Mexico. The ruins must wait. Living, beautiful, seductive
Mexico first.

Tzinzuntzan—'The Place of the Hummingbird'

No one told me about the birds. Every province has its own
special birds, like its fruit or flowers, a thousand different
fluttering, shimmering creatures, fluting, cawing, shrieking.
At Purapechas, by the end of the lake, there is a whole world,
or concentration of humming-birds, where these beetle-sized
little beauties zoom and dart about the honied trails of vine,
'cup-of-gold', or a plant called *izgujochitl*—'the flower of the
raven'. Pelicans and cormorants in Yucatan. Gaudy macaws
and parakeets flashing through the tropic groves round
Orizaba. Under the towering ash trees at Tzinzuntzan I heard
the nightingale at noon; but it turned out to be a yellow-
feathered bird, and I recalled that the Emperor Maximilian
imported two thousand nightingales from Germany: where
they, perhaps, then crossed with canaries? Everywhere, in the
mountains, in the valleys, I see those long-tailed black magpie-
like birds, so impudently friendly, which seem to address one
personally, as they flutter close to perch on the spear-tip of a
cactus or on a window-sill. The Mexicans call them 'ouraki';
in Mayan, they are 'toh'. Their song has the heart-piercing
sweetness of a blackbird's trill, with something melancholy
added, something which epitomises all Mexico at dusk.

'*O Speak to Me of Love!*'

A harem is probably the supreme example of plenty. But this is not an ample age. Along with most other of the more picturesque aspects of the Orient, polygamy is being set aside by 'progress'. The harem which Mahommed approved is now regarded as both an economic and moral issue; and in the bazaars, the story-teller's chant is shouted down by loud-speakers announcing the ever-widening interpretations of progress.

But between Tripoli and the Tunisian border, a few years ago, I heard tell of one harem which was still maintained in the traditional manner of lavish splendour. Four wives and sixty-two concubines has nothing of austerity about it. Moreover, it was housed in a palace celebrated throughout North Africa for its magnificence. I had visions of languid houris lolling on divans, of fountain courts where odalisque and eunuch revolved round the Pasha's cherished person. This might be my only chance to visit such an exotic institution. I decided to try.

Its name had long been familiar to me. Let us call it the Palais Ben Djebel. It was one of those houses around which all sorts of legends cling. There were said to be *faiences* by Goya; frescoes by Tiepolo, and European furniture looted from an Italian barque by some pirate-prince. The place had been renowned as a fabulous extravaganza—a folly. In that part of the world they say 'to build a Palais Ben Djebel', in other words, to spend wildly. There were sinister stories too. An unfaithful wife had been walled-up alive in a garden pavilion where she had kept injudicious tryst. Another had been tied to a bench in the mid-day sun 'to fade her fatal beauty'.

It had been built in the seventeenth century by some noble —a Caid, or pasha of Turkish origin, who had been made governor of the province. He had continued the Turkish custom of stocking his harem with Circassians; thus his descendants had acquired a reputation for great beauty. In the eighteenth century there had been a scandal over some jewels belonging to the Bey of Tunis. Two generations later a descendant, sumptuously dressed, appeared at a ball at the Tuileries, where he presented the Empress Eugénie with some very fine emeralds, and became a privileged, protected courtier, who speculated in real-estate, and had a street named after him in Paris; he only returned to North Africa as a decrepit, ruined roué, to die there, behind the blue lattices overlooking the roof tops which lay crumbling under the savage desert suns.

Arab buildings do not last well: even the most splendid have a transitory air about them. The nomad tent can be sensed behind the marble courts. One century of neglect gives them an air of millennial decay. So it was with the Palais Ben Djebel. While it fell to pieces, the family stagnated, poverty-stricken and forgotten. They grew old and died. The next generation lived on, in the same atmosphere of decay, and with the fatalism of the Arab race, accepted their lot. But even so, they clung to their harem, as to a principle. Indeed, this principle had, over the years, acquired the status and solidity of an old family property.

Just as, in England, the impoverished aristocracy cling at all costs to the last remnants of their feudal life, keeping, when all else has vanished, their castle, so it was here; English dukes conduct sightseers through their stately homes, the mounting toll of gate-money enabling them to preserve their inheritance for themselves and their heirs. And the last Prince Ben Djebel, in his more torrid way, had arrived at a similar compromise. At all costs the harem must be preserved: the palace might crumble, but the family pattern must remain. He took a daring step: he went into business.

According to the café proprieter, he must now be a wealthy man. As he said, four wives and sixty-two concubines argued a certain luxe.

'What exactly is his business?' I asked.

The café proprietor shrugged. 'Gun-running? Drugs?'

'Women,' said his son. 'Hand picked! He trades all over the Mediterranean.'

'Is business good?' I asked.

They both shook their heads, which is the oriental manner of saying yes.

✤   ✤   ✤

At the oasis there was some indecision as to the exact whereabouts of the place. Over there, said the Arabs, waving vaguely towards the desert. Towards the coast, said one: on the way to Ghadamés, said another. Beyond it, said a third. Finally, I appealed to the military, who knew all about the palace and its inmates, and who were sympathetic to my curiosity. It was arranged that they would provide me with a jeep and a Spahi to act as chauffeur-interpreter. There were a lot of jolly Gallic jokes about the object of my vist. Though, as the Commandant observed, just to drive up and say you wanted to see over the place—for whatever reason—would not meet with much success. The Prince suspected everyone of being connected with the police, with whom he was not on good terms. Only accredited business representatives were admitted, it seemed.

"Well, I can hardly say I want a pound of hashish or a Circassian slave,' I said.

'I often want them myself,' said a young Lieutenant, gloomily looking out across the sandy wastes.

He added that this might be quite a good moment to visit the place, saying he believed the Prince was away just now, at which the Commandant gave him a sharp look.

It was arranged that the Commandant should give me a letter for the Prince, explaining I was writing a book about Arab architecture.

'They say he is quite proud of the palace—perhaps he will be co-operative,' said the Commandant: but he did not sound hopeful.

✤　　✤　　✤

When we set off it was an oppressive, overcast morning. The Spahi, a romantic-looking young Arab, named Fardjenié, bumped the jeep at full speed from one palm clump to another, over stony fields or through cactus-hedged plantations. At last we encountered a group of Berber women working in a barley field, who knew where the palace was hidden.

More bumping across stony fields, until we approached a large clump of tall date palms and tangled vegetation surrounding a square, yellow, stone building. A number of those vicious white Kabyle dogs, whose habit it is to prowl on low rooftops, snapping at heads rather than heels, now flung themselves at us, so that it was impossible to leave the jeep. Coming nearer, we saw some mangy camels tethered to a broken-down doorway. They turned their heads, which have something of both serpent and sheep about them, and gave us a scornful stare, their long yellow teeth mincing at the cud.

Marooned in the jeep, surrounded by angry dogs, we saw no way of getting closer to the palace. But at that moment an old man shuffled into sight from nowhere. He looked more Asiatic than Arab: he might have come from one of Genghis Khan's encampments. A long, exceedingly dirty caftan draggled round his ankles. On his head was a little flat embroidered cap and two long thin moustachios drooped to his waist in Chinese fashion. In his hand he carried a most dramatic-looking curved knife. Fardjenié launched into the inevitable Arab courtesies. There was a long exchange of flowery phrases during which I picked out the Lieutenant's name, repeated several times before the dogs were stoned off, and the old man motioned us to enter the courtyard. We were in luck, said Fardjenié. The Lieutenant had been right, the Prince was away on business. The old man was his cousin, and bailiff. The mere sight of an official letter from the military had so impressed him that he raised no objections. I could go all over the palace. He unlocked the gate, and waved me towards its ruins.

The fabled palace! The harem of a thousand houris! But no echo of life reached us across the vast abandoned courts. Everywhere there was squalor and decay. Stringy vines twined round the pillars; the fountains were chipped and dry. Lizards darted, disappearing in the flick of an eye. between the cracked paving stones. In a corner, a heap of rank-smelling rags were burning slowly; a thin spiral of smoke hanging on the still air. Balconies lurched out, barely suspended by rotted beams or a twisted iron bar. There was no glass in any of the windows: faded blue shutters flapped dismally as a sudden gust of wind whipped the dust through the courts. Overhead, the birds circled uneasily, and the palm-leaves rattled metallically, a dry, scaly sound.

The old man led us from one great pillared court to the next, always empty, always ruined. He made signs to me to climb some crumbling stairs, while he and Fardjenié remained below. For Fardjenié, an Arab, the seráil or women's quarters were taboo. On the floor above I came to an interior court, a patio, open to the sky, pillared in black and white marble, with elaborate yellow and blue *faiences* covering the walls. This I took to be part of the harem; but it was as deserted as all the rest, and there were no frescoes. In the corner was a well, with some battered petrol tins attached to ropes, the first sign of everyday life. I sat down on the edge of the well and wondered which of the many doors might lead to the fabled harem.

Sitting there I remembered the story of Debureau, the great French *mime*, who, as a boy, one of a family of strolling players and acrobats, had wandered across Europe to the climax of a Command Performance in the Sultan's Seraglio. Escorted by eunuchs and viziers, they had been made to perform in what they took to be an empty hall, before a heavy brocade curtain. Behind this, although they did not know it at the time, sat the Sultan's harem, peeping through slits in the curtain. The troupe proceeded to its triumph, a human pyramid: father stood on uncle, brother supported cousin; topping the whole swaying edifice, greatly daring, the young Debureau discovered he could look over the curtain and down into the forbidden paradise below. His eyes met those of an unveiled houri. Overcome, he crashed to the ground, bringing the whole pile of relations to an ignoble finish.

※　　※　　※

The stinging sun was overhead now, and slapping away the flies, I was suddenly aware of being watched. Eyes, eyes everywhere. Eyes behind the heavy grilles, eyes peeping through cracks in the warped blue doors, eyes squinting against a chink in the panels. The harem was inspecting its visitor.

'*Bonjour!*' I said hopefully. There was no reply.

'*Arroussa!*' I tried, airing one of my few Arab phrases. *Arroussa* is alleged to be a magic password for Arab women. 'To the day of your marriage', literally, a phrase which pleases all, both past and prospective brides, whether in recollection or anticipation of that supreme occasion which, along with the birth of a son, is the sum total of an Arab woman's earthly achievement.

Suddenly a door burst open, and a very small stick-legged little Negress rushed out, her piccaninny face grinning from one coral studded ear to the other. She took the bon-bon I offered, in a pink-lined paw, and turning shy rushed away as suddenly as she had come. There were whisperings and scufflings, more moments of breathless stillness. I pretended an interest in the architecture and examined the tiles. Gradually the doors began to open, the shutters were pushed back. One by one, the harem emerged. Step by step they closed in. They did not speak, nor did I. We regarded each other obliquely, they through their veils, I through my sun glasses. Had the old man explained me, or did they take me to be a new inmate?

Now all sorts and conditions of women appeared, old, young, pretty, plain, fat, thin. Some waddled obesely, a lifetime of lolling and sweetmeats evident in their mountainous flesh. Most were enormously pregnant. There were children everywhere. One pretty little girl of about eight, whose ears were pierced, wore large safety-pins dangling from them. They were all dressed in ragged finery, with draggled draperies and greasy, snake-like locks of hair emerged from beneath their heavy veils. Some stared past me with the terrible milky blankness of trauchoma, a prevalent disease of these parts; some had already lost one eye, the other already rotting in its socket. Some squinted horribly. Some smiled broadly, displaying teeth as long and yellow as the camels: others had blackened stumps. Some of the older women dared not come out from their doorways, but lurked in the unsavoury depths, surrounded by flies, babies and cooking utensils. Gaining confidence, they began to emerge and put their pudgy, grubby hands on my brow in greeting. They were very curious about my clothes, prodding and pulling at me on all sides. No doubt my blue jeans struck them as a very meagre version of their own baggy trousers.

Over all hung an overpowering odour of stale mutton fat, and that spicy sour smell so typical of Arab countries, and which no amount of strong perfumes override. The ladies were indeed heavily perfumed. Each time they moved their tattered draperies fluttered, and a blast of jasmine or attar of roses hit

Fiesta at Chichicastenango
Yucatan: Catherwood's drawing of Mayan ruins

The Illusion

O Spea

The Invitation

The Reality

f Love!

Vernon Lee: a sketch by Sargent, 1899   Lawrence Hope: an early photograph

Pierre Loti at home

me. One by one, they shed their shyness. No more lurking in
the shadows; no more pulling of veils across their faces. Now
dozens of darkly hennaed hands plucked at me, this way and
that. With signs, we established a sort of conversation. They
showed me their rooms, their children, their needlework. They
were embroidering cushions and curtains, all sprawled across
with bold flowers, reminiscent of those found on Bessarabian
rugs. I exclaimed with exaggerated gestures of admiration
whenever I was shown anything, from a rachitic baby to a
tambourine made out of an old bully-beef tin. I produced my
camera and persuaded a few of the more emancipated to stand
still: but most of them fled at sight of the thing.

Was I mistaken, or did Fardjenié's face emerge for a moment,
stealthily, from behind a flapping shutter? No one seemed to
notice him. Perhaps I imagined it.

A sulky-looking Berber girl, who, though by far the
prettiest, seemed to be of inferior rank, was now ordered to
prepare tea. She stopped searching a small child's head and
squatting on the floor and scowling, fanned a little charcoal
brazier while another woman fetched tiny glasses which I saw
with resignation were opaque with dirt. The stoutest, most
affluent-looking matron, whom I took to be the first wife, since
she had authority over the others and wore more jewellery,
now waved imperiously towards a door which had remained
closed. An enormous key was fetched and I was led through a
darkened room to another door. This too was unlocked, to
disclose yet another, smaller shuttered room, where, in the
obscurity, I could just make out two very plump girls sitting on
the floor beside a tray of food, playing cards. They must have
been about fourteen and fifteen, and were pleasing in a bovine
way. They were fair-skinned, and their eyebrows were
elongated by lines of tattooing in elaborate dots.

'*Arroussa!*' I said once more, feeling something was required
of me. This was very well received. They beamed, and broke
into a flood of guttural phrases. But the first wife now indicated

the visit was over, and I followed her out, rather puzzled. It was not till later that I learned (from the Lieutenant) these two were the latest recruits who had not yet been, technically, incorporated into the harem, but were being, in Hollywood parlance, groomed for stardom. That is, they were being fattened up on a specially enlarging diet of oil and semolina, and were being kept away from the daylight so that their flesh would acquire the plump whiteness of asparagus. When the Prince (who was also their uncle, and, I presumed, business manager) returned from his business trip, there was to be a splendid celebration in honour of their incorporation. Evidently, whatever else fell into ruin, the harem was kept up, if not in style, at least in spirit.

After we had drunk a powerful brew of green tea, and the ladies had vied with each other, cracking and peeling nuts for me, an old Coca-Cola bottle was produced, and in a sacred hush I tasted a sickly fermented almond milk. All barriers were down now. We were fast friends. When the old man shuffled up to find me, there were angry protests and he was pushed out. But not before he had seen the Coca-Cola bottle which he fell on with an eagle's swoop. At one draught he emptied it, and belching appreciatively, looked round the crowded court. With a few graphic gestures he made it clear to me that he was not too old, when the fancy took him, to avail himself of his cousin's property. Gales of laughter mingled with cries of protest as he allowed himself to be sent packing.

We ladies of the harem—for, of course, I was quite one of them now—settled back to enjoy ourselves. Now came the *clou* of my whole tour. With obvious pride, they led me to an upper floor, by a wooden staircase so rotten that it splintered under us. We followed an arcaded gallery where the ceilings, once richly gilt and painted, were now peeling scabrously. Traces of frescoes were to be seen, but their misty smudges did not recall Tiepolo; they were, in fact, the remains of a rather meagre *toile-de-jouey* printed wallpaper which had not withstood the weather. Above, crammed into the gilded cornices, were large, ragged birds' nests, and the birds, flapping and screeching, swooped away through the gaps in the wall as we approached. Looking up, to where a ruined watch-tower gave on to an even more dilapidated loggia, I could have sworn I saw Fardjenié again, peering down on us open-mouthed and half hidden by the tumbledown balustrades. But when I looked again, the apparition had vanished.

A double door, heavily studded with nails in the Tunisian-Andalusian style, was now unlocked. With gestures of pride and apprehension too (for all of them seemed uneasy and kept glancing nervously over their shoulders) they ushered me into what was certainly the Prince's bedroom.

This holy of holies was hung with tattered Genoese velvets and, at each end, had great gilt and mirror alcove beds of the kind found chiefly in Tunisia. But now the gilding was chipped, and the mirrors were cracked across till they looked like crazy pavements. All around the walls ran a line of pegs from which hung a collection of women's clothes. There must have been a hundred or more: all kinds and colours; historic marriage costumes, stiff with gold and silver thread; shawls, scarves, Turkish trousers and boleros; pearl-embroidered, moth-eaten, stained and faded. Torn laces, limp gauzes, the striped red and yellow *foutas* of Djerba, English chintzes, batiks, satins, calicoes, and a draggled ballerina's tu-tu. Evidently the Prince kept the communal wardrobe of his charmers under personal super-vision. I imagined him lolling back in one of the alcoves, his *narghilé* beside him, absolute master of his domain, calling for this houri or that: graciously deigning to allow the favourite to enter his bed from the foot, in the traditional way, working slowly, and with symbolic humility, upwards towards the master.

I gathered there were violent scenes of jealousy, as much on account of the clothes as the Prince's favours. I was reminded of the wardrobe room of a repertory theatre where the company

bicker ceaselessly over the best costumes. With hospitable
zeal they began tearing down the different garments, holding
them against me, discussing which was best suited to my type.
On a shelf beside the bed were a dozen or more bottles of
brilliantine, and some tall silver perfume phials. Before I could
retreat, I was drenched in rose water of a particularly acrid
kind. There were fine rugs on the floor, but they were torn and
threadbare. Beside a pair of Italian cabinets, inlaid with
tortoiseshell and ivory, leaned a man's bicycle. In the corner of
the room stood a large red factory time-clock. Perhaps with
sixty-two concubines, to say nothing of four wives, the Prince
found it best to apportion out his favours scrupulously.
Following my eyes, the ladies surged round, punched it
expertly, and presented me with the disgorged ticket. '1·45'
it read.

'Heavens! I must fly! I shall be terribly late for luncheon,'
I heard myself saying. The phrase rang oddly through the
Prince's bedroom. Yet the luncheon tables of civilization are
always calling us back. . . .

'For I have measured out my life in coffee spoons,' as
T. S. Eliot says, somewhere.

The harem followed me, pantomiming their grief, their hope
that I would stay on among them. Indeed, I think they would
have welcomed any stranger, waiving their jealousies in the
pleasures of a distraction. Some of them, I learned later, had
never even seen a car, or visited the nearest oasis. Some had
never left the palace: some had been born there: none of them
could read or write. I was the first foreign woman they had ever
seen. They surrounded me, holding my hands lovingly . . .
Bislemmah! Goodbye! They placed their auburn fingers on
their lips in the ritual gesture of farewell, as I emptied my bag,
to find souvenirs for them. A packet of coloured-headed pins
threw the first wife into transports of delight. I exchanged an
eyebrow pencil for a little copper jar of Kohl. The best kind
is said to be made from pulverized bats, and I longed to ask

if this was so. My lipstick, 'Formal Red', I was reserving for the sulky Berber girl who had made the tea, but she was nowhere to be seen.

Downstairs in the courtyard I found the old man dozing on a straw mat. There was no sign of Fardjenié: but while I was stacking my things in the jeep, he came out from a doorway across the court followed by the Berber girl. Like all her race, she was not veiled. Their nomad ways and brazenly exposed faces have given them a hussy's reputation. Did she exchange a farewell glance with Fardjenié? Their expressive faces told me nothing, but I thought the Spahi looked gloomy.

As we drove off I saw the ruined balconies were crowded. The harem were all there, recklessly, to watch us leave. I waved. They waved back. *Bislemmah!* The big black birds circled overhead, the dogs raced yelping beside our wheels, and the last flutter of scarves was lost behind the cactus hedges.

On the way back, Fardjenié recounted a number of details of home life at the Palais Ben Djebel. No doubt the Berber girl had been persuaded to talk. It seemed that the Prince seldom mixed business with pleasure, and the inhabitants of the place had little connection with his trading enterprises; they were elsewhere. . . . Most of the harem I had encountered were of his own family: his wives, daughters and slaves; the families of his brothers or cousins. Some were his own favourites said Fardjenié. There were so many women . . . it was difficult to say which was which. This was a traditional household. The women led completely sequestered lives, and had few amusements. They were not like modern girls, said Fardjenié. He sighed, profoundly. 'Our visit—*your* visit,' he corrected himself, 'will be remembered for ever.'

'Well, *I* shall never forget it,' I replied.

He gave me a sidelong glance from his treacle-soft eyes, which were suddenly spiteful. After some miles of cross-country bumping, he burst out bitterly.

'I have heard tell of the Palais Ben Djebel ever since I was a little boy. My father used to talk about the Prince's harem. My grandfather too. . . . Every man dreamed of possessing such a one. . . . It was all hearsay, to them. . . . But I have seen it!'

He gave me another spiteful glance, and I knew that I had shattered the illusions of his youth.

Undulators and Adulators

The café looked like any other; it was small and dirty and dark, and getting darker, for it was dusk, and the electricity had broken down. A ha'penny dip guttered in the corner, where a decrepit Arab fanned a little brazier for the clients' tea and coffee. Gradually the place filled up. Some elegantly dressed elderly men—rich merchants, I afterward learned—came in followed by what appeared to be young pages, beautiful, very dark-skinned boys. Some wore elaborate white turbans, most of them were veiled like houris, or Touaregs. Over the thick folds, they cast limpid glances at our table. One group was followed by a tame sheep. A few pompous-looking old men sat stiffly in the corner and were obviously standing treat for several shy-looking creatures from the desert, I guessed, and new to the city. Presently the flower-vendors came round and did a brisk trade with the little jasmine bouquets which are typical of Tunis. The starry flowers are mounted on pine needles, like tightly furled umbrellas: gradually they unfold, the spokes open, umbrella-like, and the little bouquets spread out, perfumed toys. Tunisians love this plaything, and in the cool of the evening you will see soldiers, policemen, taxi-drivers and beggars all savouring them voluptuously. In the café, the boys were sniffing them in ecstasy, or pinning them into their turbans, where they spread out over their dusky cheeks in a most enticing way. There was a lot of coming and going, and a strongly family or tribal atmosphere.

This was the favourite meeting-place of the Ouarglis and

their friends, I learned. In Tunis the best servants are Ouarglis. They come up from their country on the edge of the Sahara, in eastern Algeria, to work in the cities, but keep very much to themselves, a lone community. They are markedly effeminate in both appearance and bearing; but it is the delicate, romantic effeminacy often found among Arab men. It has nothing of the degeneracy associated with over-femininity in the West, and watching them, you are reminded how small a place women have ever played in Arab civilization. If they bred sons they were ensured a respected old age. Otherwise, after a few brief seasons of delight—the rest was silence.

The Ouarglis appeared to be a world of their own, enclosed and self-sufficient. They have their own Caïd, who ruled over them with considerable indulgence, I fancy. Their own cafés and caravanserais, or hostels, were hidden away in the labyrinthine souks. Their *Bureau de Placement*, or Registry Office, was always crowded with these graceful, coquettish creatures, looking for situations as cooks or house-boys. I reflected how welcome they would be in Europe or America.

The night we chanced on their café, somebody was celebrating something—I never knew what—and there were to be dancers and musicians. The Ouarglis are famous for their dancing, which it is claimed, can rival that of the Ouled Näils. But whereas the Ouled Näil women are traditional prostitutes, their costumes, beauty and sensual delights celebrated all over North Africa, the Ouarglis are strictly amateurs, only dancing among themselves, with no calculated tourist effects. Straying into their café, being allowed to stay, all this was because my companion, a Turk, was known to the establishment. We lurked in the darkest corner and watched. There were the endless, monotonous, yet strangely stimulating songs of Arab tradition: the plaintive flute, the hot, savage drum-beats of the *derboulka*, all Africa in its rhythm, a sort of lute, and a toy violin daubed with gold paint and played across the knee.

Sometimes the musicians sang, hurling a long thread of melody above the café's din.

The Ouarglis began to dance; undulating, vibrating rather than moving. Their rich elderly adorers looked on entranced. These persons are prosperous—mostly merchants from the same part of the world. They trade in ostrich plumes, dates, and particularly, ostrich marrow fat, considered an infallible cure for rheumatism. Lately they have been much disturbed by bootlegging competition, a black-market substitute made from donkey's marrow. Not at *all* the same thing, I was told, heads shaken in condemnation.

The merchants lapsed in silence again, their eyes following the dancers' undulations. But soon, these languorous delights were broken up by the arrival of their celebrated teacher, Amarr Ould Djella, famous all across North Africa. From the Tiznit dancers of Morocco to those of the Kerkenneh Isles, Amarr was respected. The Ouled Näils used to send their star performers to him for coaching (so did Egyptian impresarios perfecting their best belly-dancers, before Cairene night-life was cleaned up). He came across to us, and accepted an English cigarette. He was about fifty—small, pale, finicky, with cat-like gestures, and was wrapped in a large European over-coat under which some gaudy rags draggled round his white tennis shoes. He looked like one of those seedy tumblers who entertain provincial theatre queues.

When he stood up to dance, and removed his overcoat, I was reminded of the Widow Twankey. He wore an electric-blue, long-sleeved under-vest, his turban had worked askew, and low round his hips a dazzling sequin belt was safety-pinned to a flaming salmon-pink satin skirt. But when he began to dance, there was no more of the grotesque pantomime droll. The shoddy costume, the tennis shoes, the safety-pins . . . all faded. It was the fabled Orient, Haroun Al Raschid's dancer, Salome and her seven veils; all seduction, all provocation, the wiles of the flesh incarnate. He danced the traditional slow, almost static dances, where only head and neck sway; the curious fluttering finger and wrist dance of the Ouled Näils, and the immemorial love-dances of the East, where writhing muscles and erotic belly swayings leave nothing unsaid, but which were, in this instance, rather hampered by the under-vest.

The circle of Ouarglis closed in, watching, enthralled. The ha'penny dip gleamed feebly on the rapt faces. The coffee pots boiled over unchecked; only the sheep seemed unmoved by the frenzies and dozed in a corner.

✤ ✤ ✤

Next day, we were invited to the Ouarglis caravanserai, a big covered courtyard, where many of them lived and received their friends in little cells opening off the square. Amarr was to be there giving a lesson to some particularly promising young dancer. It was a Thursday, generally the Ouarglis servants' afternoon off. Most of them repair to the caravanserai, where a convent, rather than monastery, atmosphere prevailed (the sort of Venetian convent of which Casanova wrote: a worldly scene); much chatter and comings and goings of visitors and inmates; tiffs and reconciliations. Newcomers up from their home-town were sitting round, regaling the boys with family news. There were the usual refreshments—tea, the intoxicating green Arab tea, and slender pipes for opium, or *kef,* which though strictly speaking, proscribed, is still sometimes enjoyed. Its sickly, unmistakable smell hung on the air. Their Cäid arrived, and the traditional pot of basil was placed before him. This is a refinement of taste, of living, found in many Arab countries, where it is quite customary to enter a café and order a glass of water and a bouquet, or a pot of basil. The Arab is often content to sit contemplating a plant, nourished on beauty, in place of buns.

The orchestra filed in, but now, primed for the photographs

we wished to take, they were a colourless band, transformed
by what they proudly considered a more photogenic get-up—
gents' natty suitings. Amarr arrived, his blue vest and sequin
skirt glittering in the sunlight which filtered through the
trellised vines. The new pupil had the same feline grace of all
his tribe; his eye-lids curved like scimitars above the muffling
white veils. He was Valentino and Salome in one, and everyone
suddenly looked faint with longing. . . .

The lesson began. Amarr led, the pupil followed, turning
and twisting, shuffling and posturing. The musicians changed
their beat, and Amarr slashed his way through a fiery sabre
dance. The new pupil panted after him, watching every step.
Do it this way—try it again! One! Two! One! Two! I
seemed to hear all the echoes of the many great teachers I have
watched. Kesschinskayas's class in Paris. *Ras! Dva! Tri!*
Simienova rehearsing in a classroom of the Bolshoi Theatre of
Moscow. Marie Rambert at the Ballet Club. . . . The echoes
merged with the one, two, three, hop, of my first dancing-class
polkas.

The lesson lasted a full two hours. Amarr is a perfectionist,
giving value for money. Times were hard he said, and pupils
were fewer, poorer. He was compelled to eke out his living by
taking in washing (shades of the Widow Twankey once more).
After the lesson he obliged with a solo dance—one of his star
turns. Balanced on glass tumblers, a pitcher poised on his head,
he executed a particularly erotic number. The rich merchants
applauded frenziedly, and money rained round. Bowing right
and left, like a *prima ballerina assoluta*, waving and smiling his
thanks, Amarr backed gracefully out of the ring taking his pupil
with him. The audience repaired to their cells with their
admirers. Doors slammed shut. It was time to go. We left
Amarr and his pupil reposing in one of the more elaborate
cells, a sort of star's dressing-room, adorned with pictures,
mirrors, flowers, and dominated by a large velvet covered
sofa, *style* Louis-Philippe. There they would repose after

their efforts, sip tea, gossip, and discuss what sort of future lay in store for an Ouargli dancing boy today. But in North Africa, that today is already yesterday. How much traditionalism will survive, tomorrow, I wonder?

13

Vernon Lee's Italy

When in 1944 the tide of destruction swept up Italy, bull-dozing its way through civilization's heritage and tourist panoramas alike, my mind turned often to the writings of Vernon Lee. Her best work was as an essayist—an essayist of Europe, and best of all, of Italy. But she has become as neglected, as unfashionable as her subject—provincial Italy. The petrol-fed overtones of more exotic travellers, ever further and wilder, drowned her elegiac undertones. And she has some fearful habits, sprinkling her prose with 'tis and nay: indulging in long macaroni-twists of phrase, wildly bracketed and dashed, which only the most willing can disentangle. Her convolutions are Mandarin English at its most florid; yet suddenly confounded by a single sharply tailored line. Some of her work is as ornamented as a parasol handle by Fabergé, and has that same power to irritate, or charm.

There was a time about 1900 when she charmed not only an eclectic few, but a wide public who read her contributions to the *Yellow Book*, the *Westminster*, and other periodicals, or snatched her reprinted works in the Tauchnitz edition, on their travels.

> 'No, the book
>   Which noticed how the wall-growths wave', said she,
> 'Was not by Ruskin.'
>   I said 'Vernon Lee?'

Thus Browning, in *Asolando*; and his glancing allusion was a tribute. They were neighbours in Florence, and the poet had a great admiration for her erudition, and above all, for her imaginative perception, her sense of the Italian scene. The Genus Loci. 'The emotion of Italy', she calls it herself, speaking of the way in which countries, like people, have each their own individual way of being lovable and hateful.

Her love and understanding of Italy was no blinkered craze, no case of 'what know they of England who only England know'. She was one of that rare, fast-vanishing type of intellectual who is at home in, not just conversant with, the culture of many different countries. She could express herself as finely in French as in German. She read Dante as she read Plato, in the original. Her knowledge of music was as profound as her studies of aesthetics.

But it is in her power of conveying the Genus Loci that she excels. She has an objective clarity, where so many others are bogged in subjectivity. She is not a landscape painter, for though she often writes scenically, she usually discusses the philosophy, literature and flavour of the place, and at all times, discovers its essential spirit. She knew and sensed so many aspects of the European scene. Tame scenes, perhaps, in the light of latter-day rangings: but perfect, for all their pastel-toned, small perspectives.

Switzerland: the prim, reasonable peace of Lavater's house at Zurich. The Germany of little gingerbread Bavarian villages, with Christmas angels and woolly lambs on toothpick legs; dark Thuringian forests; tiny formal gardens, the Prinzes-sinnen-Garten of some Margrave's Courtlet. France: the early-Corot landscape; Aucassin's spectral castle at Beaucaire, under a sirocco sky. The endless avenues of the Burgundian table-land. The mangy outskirts of Paris. All the shades and half shades of grey spread over shutters, walls and roofs. Straggling northern villages, with their 'close-fisted *cossu* middle-class air, seemingly inhabited not by peasants, but by notaries and *receveurs'*. Yes, she sensed France. England, also. The harsh and grating North, with its livid light, its damp; or dusty, social

Surrey. But Italy—'have I really cared for any other country?' she asked. I think not.

In her writings of Italy there is always a note of fulfilment, of beatitude. Her pen skims along, imbued with a special grace, a sort of reverential gusto. Listen to her on Rome—the Rome of her childhood, in the last splendid years of temporal power. She recalls how she was wakened early, dressed by candlelight, in black clothes, belonging to her elders, and crushed into a two-seater cab,

> to St. Peter's, where I waited for hours, among the knees of veiled and black-dressed ladies: hours that seemed an endless dream under this immense cupola, shimmering blue and white and gold, when the sunbeams, through a haze of incense, struck upon the huge golden letters 'Tu es Petrus'. Endless, endless: until at last there echoed through the vastness of the place the quavering notes of the singers, the shrill blast of the trumpets; and then became visible, moving above the heads, above the sheen of the bayonets and the halberds, the great fans of ostrich feathers, the golden tassels of the gently swaying throne, the white splendour of the pontifical robes and jewels. The trumpets shrilled through the cupola, the incense rose in great blue wreaths. I thought of King Solomon, when (as I had read in the Arabian Nights) he passed in review the legions of angels and djins and furies, obedient to the power of the ring.

There was another Rome, degenerate and stale. She knew that, too.

> This dreary, horrible Rome of the popes: this warm, wet place with its sordid houses, its ruins embedded in filth and nettles; its tawdry stuffy churches filled with snuffling monks, and jig-quavering of strange, cracked, sickening-sweet voices; its whole atmosphere of decay and sloth, as of a great marsh-pond, sprinkled with bright green weed, and starred with flaunting nauseous yellow lilies.

But Tuscany was her home: I think she analysed it even

better than the rest of Italy. Speaking of the connection between a country and its art, she writes:

> A very Tuscan, or rather, a very Florentine day. Beauty, exquisiteness and serenity; but not without austerity carried to a distinct bitingness. And this is the quality which we find again in all very characteristic Tuscan art ... Vitae Nuova, the really great (not merely historically interesting) passages of the Divine Comedy, and the popular songs of Tigris' collection are as much the outcome of these Tuscan mountains and hills as any picture in which we recognise their outline and colours.

She speaks of it being a moving, changing landscape:

> massed into harmonious and ever changing groups. Ever changing, as you move, hills rising and sinking as you mount or descend, furling and unfurling as you go to the right or to the left, valleys and ravines opening or closing up, the whole country altering, so to speak, its attitude and gesture as quickly, almost, and with quite as perfect consecutiveness as does a great cathedral when you walk round it. And for this reason, never letting you rest; keeping you also in movement, feet, eyes, and fancy.

To quote her on Italy would be to fill many books. She conjures many aspects. The petty principalities of Stendhal's Duchess. The heroic land of Meredith's Vittoria. Sad, malarious little towns of the Maremma. The elegant classicism of Claude or Vernet. Tiepolo's sugar-icing. The overgrown forgotten gardens of Tuscany, with noble arms emblazoned on their great gates . . . gates leading nowhere.

Hers was no mere tourisme. She resented what she called the prostitution of Italy to idle strangers. (How she would have abhorred the fleshy abandon of today's Lido or Hollywood's invasion of Rome, by way of Cinecitta.) Herself, at times, an apparently superficial writer, she grudged the tourists' passing enthusiasms. Hers was based deep in thought and emotion, the outcome of a contemplative nature stirred to action only by a desire for wider knowledge. She was well aware of her good fortune, in possessing modest means which gave her leisure to discover herself, and to avoid the cheaper competitions of wage-earning. And although she craved personal success, and liked to display her conversational fireworks, holding the floor ruthlessly, in her work, she was diffident to the point of deprecation. She never pushed it as she sometimes pushed her personality.

Vernon Lee was a pseudonym. Her name was Violet Paget. She was born in 1856 and died in 1935. She was a precocious child, surrounded by doting elders. Her half-brother Eugène Lee-Hamilton (whose writings also appeared in the *Yellow Book*) was many years her senior. Her early life was spent in travel, with little or no schooling, but very much education. After a brief and disenchanted spell in Kensington she settled abroad, living mostly in Italy. Her earliest specialised studies were on various aspects of the eighteenth century, in Italy; minor musicians, the *Fiabe* of Carlo Gozzi and such.

I imagine her life was unrestricted, but not undisciplined. Much to-ing and fro-ing from schloss to villa, eager friendships, voluminous correspondence of her era, and many expeditions, undertaken in a mood of almost sacred sight-seeing. I imagine her, in her hey-day, established, yet somehow not rooted; a sort of perpetual picnicker, for ever touring, jaunting, questing, always on the move, greedy for those sights and sounds which, by her own alchemy, she transmuted from a Baedeker-like mass into an individual *salmagundi*. My mind's eye sees her as a solitary figure, academic and remote, on some romantic stretch of road, perhaps the Appian way, in the shade of an ilex tree, her bicycle beside her, her plaid golf-cape—the perfect period piece—spread around. Her severe 'English Mees' appearance belied the truth, testified by several of her contemporaries, that she was, in fact, a capricious, even spectacular traveller. Her bicycle tours sometimes acquired a circus air, since she insisted on being followed by a carriage, containing several extra pairs of boots and the elegant boot-trees she affected. She was a plain woman, but justly proud of her well-shaped feet.

Her span of life was wide. A child in the Rome of the Rissorgimente. The pupil of one who remembered how Cimarosa sang his own comic songs: the benefactor who stretched out a hand to help the tattered, dying Ouida: the clear-sighted critic who summed up D'Annunzio: a tired woman who outlived her generation: though her writings prove how ageless her mind remained: ageless, but not dateless. She died in an Italy which had crystallised in Fascism.

She died in time. The desolation of the 1914–18 war had appalled her. She wrote of world affairs, as in *Satan the Waster*, with surprising surety. She could come out of her academic shell when she chose. She mourned the 'wrecked landscape of the human soul'. In her essay *In Time of War*, written in 1925, she speaks with bitterness of the spiritual vandalism on which the stay-at-homes of all nations (with priests and poets and sages at their head) have been incessantly engaged. Speaking of certain German towns she writes: 'For though they stand intact in the material world the thought of them has been sacked, burnt, defiled, ten thousand times over by millions of indignant wills; and by imaginative thirsting for reprisals.' Perhaps later holocausts purge much of this reprisal-spirit, but at a fearful price. I am glad she was spared the bulletins of World War II which told coldly, as we accepted calmly, the awful total of each day's progress towards peace.

Vernon Lee wrote much that was not topographical. Essays in a philosophical and critical strain. Abstruse themes with such titles as *Vital Lies: studies of some recent varieties of Obscurantism. Hortus Vitae. Euphorion: essays on the Renaissance.* Her treatises on aesthetics were considered by the late Roger Fry to be a rare and valuable contribution to this subject. While Mr. Lane, of the Bodley Head, is said to have been more proud of being her publisher than all the rest of his

illustrious band. She wrote some fiction too. *Hauntings*, and
Pope Jacynth, and *Vanitas*; *Polite Stories*, of which one, *The
Legend of Madame Krasinska*, is a magnificently macabre story.
Her best fiction always has this supernatural tinge. When she
is social or contemporary, as in *Lady Tal*, she is unreal and
strained, and poorly influenced by Henry James. But two of her
stories of the supernatural linger in my mind; they are fore-
runners of the *Berkeley Square* theme; lovers separated by the
centuries; beautifully told, oddly evil; strong, possessive
stories, utterly unexpected from the cerebral and finnicky
author of *Studies in Obscurantism*, or *An Empirical Study of
Emotion and Imaginative Response to Music*.

She had humour, and wit too, although I must admit she
sometimes has a tiresomely pixie touch, which is possibly more
eloquent of her period than her personality. But at her best, she
enchants. Here she is in a letter to Maurice Baring, expounding
her theory that great art always holds back—is never forth-
coming. Apropos Wagner she is devitalised by his music 'as
by the contemplation of a slug'. She speaks of how he turns
everything into a process of gloating, and of his quality of
auto-religion: 'The element of priesthood in it all, like English
people contemplating their hat-linings in Church, their prudery
about the name of God, as if it were that of some sanitary or
medical applicance, or like modern Catholics (for I'm sure the
Middle Ages were different) refusal to smile at the sight of a
wax Madonna's garters.'

How neatly she sums up her old-maid's life, her unpre-
possessing qualities which condemned her to 'pine on a perch'.
Speaking of Maurice Baring's writing, she praises his 'bony,
dry style; a blessing after so much lusciousness (sleepy pears
with wasps hidden in them!)' with which she had perfectly
described the lushly decadent style of her contemporaries. In
the main, she avoided other writers. She thought their work
destroyed their personalities. In another letter to Maurice
Baring, dated 1906, she writes:

people nowadays write so well, when they do write well, that their human personality is apt to be mere dregs in the sieve. That's why I avoid writers: 'tis a bad trade exhausting people of their better qualities and replacing them by wicked vanities.... Look at Barres and D'Annunzio: they think because they write. When they don't write, they don't think—worth thinking of— at all.

❖   ❖   ❖

There has been little written about Vernon Lee, either as a woman, or a writer. She is glimpsed in the letters and memories of her hey-day: in the autobiographies of Dame Ethel Smyth and Maurice Baring, and in a privately printed memoir. On her death it was found she had forbidden a biography. One wonders why. There are few people less qualified to write about her than myself, for I never knew her. Only my interest in her, and my abiding pleasure in her writings gives me, I hope, the right to recall her to some, or perhaps introduce her to others. Although I never knew her, she is one of the legends of my life. Her name and face were as familiar to me before I could read. My earliest picture books were old bundles of the *Studio*, dating back to my mother's girlhood. I pored over Brangwyn's murals, Lazlo's sycophantic portraits, and art nouveau furniture. One picture haunted me. It was a portrait, drawn in red chalk. It was not like any other face. The mannish cloth hat and stiff collar beloved of the emancipated woman of the 'nineties bewildered me. 'Vernon Lee', read Nanny, with finality, in answer to my tireless questioning. The androgynous name hung on the ear unforgettably, but gave no clue. Lady— gentleman? Nanny couldn't say. A John Sargent sketch in sanguine, for that's what it was, meant nothing to her. She was in her element, however, when I turned the page, and came to the penny-dreadful dramatics of Arnold Böecklin's sirens.

Years later, when I discovered Vernon Lee's travel books,

such as *The Tower of the Mirrors*, or *The Genus Loci*, and these had disclosed to me the escapist joys of Abroad, I returned to the Sargent portrait, and found it fitted the personality her writings evoked. It was a long, horse-face, freckled, it seemed, and bonily intelligent, framed by wisps of sandy, or was it greyish hair? Sargent's facile, yet incisive sketch caught the narrowed eyes gleaming out, sidelong and quizzical; impersonal, unfeminine, even, in their air of dispassionate observation—of onlooking, rather than participating in the human comedy.

Or did she find it a tragedy? I rather think she did, and that the portrait was no guide to one side of her nature. Her looks belied her. She appeared an angular, governessy creature, spinster-sharp and didactic. But she was a shy, tormented, over-loving soul, possessive, and clumsy, whose lack of social tact crashed one Eden after the next. According to Dame Ethel Smyth, who knew and understood her well, she made 'many ill-conceived excursions into the inner life of someone she adored'. Her tyrannical cults for first one person, then the next, led to irretrievable emotional disasters. But she could not learn restraint.

At her Florentine villa, Il Palmerino, she lived for many years with her brother Eugène, who at that time was a complete invalid. After remaining immobile with spinal trouble for twenty years, he was suddenly miraculously cured, his first action being to walk up Vesuvius, thus bearing out the family reputation for oddity. A constant stream of visitors found her hospitality a doubtful joy. Fevered, all-night debates on aesthetic subjects were conducted in a professional manner, Vernon Lee's thin, high-pitched voice dominating the rest. A Graeco-Roman bust would be analyzed from its 'objective-, picture-, architecture-, statue aspect', as well as its 'physio-logical-psychological' one. Apart from all this *brouhaha* of emotion and intellect, there was an arid atmosphere; such very high-thinking had its attendant low living. Meagre rations, draughts; the cook's repertoire of traditional Florentine dishes such as tongue stewed in chocolate, or the claws of a bird of prey, embedded in an omelette.

It grieves me not to have known her, since once I was her neighbour. Such a woman would have been worth all the uproar, all the omelettes. After school I was sent out to Florence and found her name still fluttered the tea-tables of the Tornabuoni. Her villa was near ours, hung on the hillside, above the city. Squelching through the mud, or dragging through the dust, on our daily, ritualistic breather, we often passed the twisted olives and broken stone walls that led to Il Palmerino. 'We simply must go and see Miss Paget,' became a mechanical utterance with our chaperone. Secretly, I fancy she feared this formidable personality, who could have had little time or inclination for *bäckfisch* and their guardians. But time passed, and we never went there. It was too wet. It was too hot. We had errands in the town. She was getting very deaf. I was too shy to press forward. She was becoming a recluse. She was away. . . . She was dead. To me, she has remained a legend.

14

Loti in Loti-land

Just as every city has its moment in time, so it has its painter or poet who best interprets it to the rest of the world: impossible to imagine the endless birch forests of Russia without peopling them with Turgenev characters. Even the least classical tourist sun-bathing in the Aegean recalls a Byronic distillation. Any walk through the English country-side of ploughed fields and misty hills recalls Cobbett, or Marvell; the scene seems awaiting the landed gentry of Gainsborough's family groups, debonair squires leaning on stiles, beside button-eyed wives, wispy little girls and frolicking gun-dogs. This is their setting: they are stamped on it for posterity, despite the pylons and the bungalows.

So with Istanbul today. When present progress has been admired, and all the historic panorama unwound, it is not the grandeurs of Byzantium and the 'Greens and the Blues' that come first to mind nor Lady Mary Wortley Montagu's pawky accounts of the Ottoman court, but rather Pierre Loti's now unfashionable writings—*Aziyadé* of course, and *Fantôme d'Orient*, his finest piece of evocation. Loti found his perfect subject in this city; his melancholy genius, or rather his genius for poetic melancholy, is the city's eternal core, whether its whole goes by the name of Constantinople, Stamboul, or Istanbul.

'Loti?' a deprecating half-smile: 'I'm afraid I haven't read him since I was at school.' This is the reaction today: although both Anatole France and Courteline stoutly proclaimed him, without question, the greatest living French writer of their day,

Anatole France also describing him as *'le sublime illettré'*. And Louis Barthou: 'Posterity has begun for Pierre Loti. He has been assessed. . . . As long as there are lands and seas, forests, deserts, rivers, mountains, and seasons, the name of Pierre Loti will live. . . . As long as men suffer and love, and dread death, too. His genius springs from a double source: nature and the heart. It is because he has written of them with such incomparable art that he remains eternal.' And Gide declared, *'Grâce détendue, retombée, qui se trouve chez Loti.'* All the unfashionable adjectives, sublime, noble, incomparable, poignant, belong to Loti. His cumulative artistry, his particular charm, overcome whole chunks of bathos. It doesn't matter: we skip, and then, coming to a passage of subtle evocation, we are held entranced.

When I returned to Istanbul after a gap of seven years, I found myself drawn once again into the web of nostalgia which is this city's secret. However much the surface changes, in spite of grinding trams and roaring American taxis, blaring radios and crops of new buildings mushrooming up across those empty wastes which are perpetual reminders of the Asiatic hinterland, the spirit of the city, its skyline of mosque and minaret and cyprus soaring up from Marmora, or Bosphorus, or Corne d'Or—while the chailak, a bird of prey, wheels overhead—this remains forever Loti-land.

Pierre Loti's nature responded to and found a response in its romantic decay. He loved its crumbling splendours, savoured its spectral beauty, listened for its ghostly echoes— ghostly, even in his day. He liked to think he regretted its past glories, but what he really enjoyed was the regret. In Loti's writings there is always this voluptuous abandonment to nostalgia. He found his perfect subject when the ship on which he was serving as an ensign sailed up the Dardenelles to anchor off Seraglio Point. This was in 1877: for the last ten years the young Louis-Marie-Julien Viaud to give him his real name, had been in the French navy; his voyages had already taken him to Brazil, the Pacific, Tahiti, and Sénégal, from which he later derived several of his best-known novels; but it was Turkey which inspired his finest work. From this first impact came *Aziyadé*, which is, in substance, autobiographical; it tells of his liaison with the little Circassian Kadine who escaped from a harem to live a brief idyll in the arms of the giaour and then to pine and die, abandoned. A return to Constantinople, many years later, inspired its sequel, *Fantôme d'Orient*; and his last visit, the coda, *Suprêmes Visions d'Orient*, written thirty years after the fabulous city first rose up out of the Marmora before his dazzled eyes.

It was more than a city he sensed then: it was a whole way of life and a people, which cast a spell over him for the rest of his days.

Loti was at his best as a subjective traveller, turning his foregrounds into backgrounds for his tragic loves. *Le Mariage de Loti, le Roman d'un Spahi, Aziyadé, Fleurs d'Ennui*, all these are Loti seeing himself in the various landscapes. He moves through the enchanted scenes, Loti in Loti-land, always seeking the plaintive undertones, as minor in key as the Oriental *mélopées* he loved, always draining an embittered cup to the dregs, but savouring it in delicious sips, choosing his sorrows with the deliberation others reserve for their pleasures. In Turkey, the tragi-comedy reached its apogee, and we see Loti going with self-conscious melancholy through the deserted streets of the Phanar, to hear the fifth, or evening, prayer at the Mehmet Fatih mosque; choosing the *mise en scène* with a theatrical sense; lingering in the shadowy cypress-planted courtyard; luxuriating in the muezzin's chant, that '*gémissement religieux, lugubre à faire frémir*', as it floated out from the spear-like minarets, to hang, vibrating, on the vapours of the chill night air; going, in positive ecstasies of grief, to search out the *stelé* of his lost love, somewhere among the forests of graves and cypresses beyond the Byzantine walls, graves which he describes as 'sunk in solitude, drunk with silence'.

Loti

Loti longed to be part of the great stream of Eastern life: the crowds which surged through the narrow, vine-swagged street markets of Tophane or Kum Kapou were, to him, a life-giving stream into which he plunged. The boatmen, hamils, beggars, Turcomen, Persians or Albanians who lay sprawled along the harbour, then, as now, brawling, sleeping, jesting—these people had, for him, an irresistible allure. In the beginning he deliberately chose a humble milieu in preference to the more westernised élite, learning the language of the people, their ways and legends. By every means he sought to identify himself with this land of his predilection, and he found a warm response; there were no reserves on either side—although it must be admitted that Loti's rôle was a favoured one. He was always the pasha of, yet not quite of, the circle; not bound by local horizons, however much he might appear, even to himself, to crave them. Perhaps this detachment gave him sharper appreciations; perhaps, too, it gave the Turks an equally lively realisation of Loti's value among them, not only as an ardent Turcophile, but as a world-famous man of letters and, even in the beginning, an officer of the puissant Allied fleet then patrolling Turkish waters. In any case, his peccadilloes and *jeux* were observed with indulgence by both small fry and government officials.

Of all the many aspects of Moslem life which Loti sought to penetrate, it was those hours of retreat, of contemplation and withdrawal which he most treasured. Such stretches of deliberate, voluptuous nothingness—*kef*, to the Arabs—are known to all Eastern peoples: the Turks call it *rahat*; it is the quintessential Oriental retreat from a too-pressing reality. Again and again in his writings Loti returns to the enchantment of those timeless hours becalmed in stillness, in drifts of dreams, forming and re-forming, nebulous as the smoke rising from his *narghilyé*. In today's jargon it would be called escapism: but to Loti, who fled reality down the years, it was Elysium.

In Turkey, he found it easily enough. In the haze of the

hammam; beside some cypress-shaded graveyard; or in some small café with a terrace overlooking a sunset, such as one he loved beside the Green Mosque at Broussa; or, equally, in the splendours such as those he describes, when, as guest of Izeddin-Ali-effendi, he is offered a traditional Turkish night's entertainment in the *selamlik*, or men's quarters of a princely establishment. Here, with a refinement of luxury, there is no feasting, no riotous living, but a gathering of men, centred round the glowing copper mangal, stretched on divans, in their fur-lined caftans, each with their long jasmine-stemmed *tchibouk*, or *narghilyé*, to pass the long winter's night together, in stillness, in *rahat*, 'this rêverie which is not thought, which is more than feeling, and which no word expresses'. Timeless hours, neither haunted by the past, nor shadowed by the future, but filled with an animal sense of well-being. For Loti, with all his curiously pagan horror of death, these hours gave him the longed-for illusion that time stood still. They were perhaps the real secret of his hunger for the East. Later, he tried to introduce such evenings among his Western friends, but they only found it a picturesque novelty, and soon began to fidget.

Even in the house for lovers' meeting at Eyüp, living what was the supreme adventure of his life, he was savouring *rahat* with the same abandon as his amorous transports. 'Only the Oriental knows how to live inwardly, within himself, his home', he writes longingly. And in a letter describing the life at Eyüp he goes on, 'it was so good to be there, far away from everyone, everything, so still, so peaceful, so alone . . . (*le bien-être égoïste du chez soi*). I would lock our door and sit cross-legged, while Achmet my servant prepared two *narghilyés*, one for me, the other for himself. Aziyadé's voice sounded a sombre note as she sang the song of the djinns, striking her little drum, which was hung with twinkling coins. As the smoke began to rise slowly in bluish spirals I would find myself, little by little, forgetting all the tragic realities of human life.'

Loti

Yes, Aziyadé's lover was, first of all, an escapist.

❖   ❖   ❖

The curiously obsessive force of Loti's writing is such that he still seems to pervade Stamboul. He is that quiet form sitting by the dervishes' cells, at the Sokullu Mehmet Pacha mosque; he is that figure posing dramatically before an itinerant photographer's canvas backcloth painted with the crescent of Islam. He is the loiterer in the glittering souks: his is the face that stares down on the crowd from the bird-cage-like yoghourt kiosque in the Great Bazaar. I see him in the dappled shade of any street café, at Beyazit, or the Atmëidan. He sits there, the eternal revenant, a faintly self-conscious figure, at once actor and audience, and greatly enjoying his own performance. He wears a fez, of course, and toys with an amber chaplet. He is handsome: *bel homme*, in that rather pronounced-featured manner of his age. He has the sumptuous moustaches and fine dark eyes of the *carte-postale* hero; eyes which were, in the words of a friend, 'the tragic, questioning eyes of a suffering animal, haunting in their pathos'. Fascinating, too.

He was an irresistible figure in the 'nineties, not only to inexperienced, untravelled girls who might be expected to revel in armchair excursions and tantalising mixtures of spirit and flesh ('It was reserved for Pierre Loti to make us savour—to the point of drunknenness, of delirium, of stupor, even, the bitter flavour of exotic loves', wrote Anatole France, quite beside himself, and voicing his contemporaries), but *mondaine* hostesses in palmy salons were spellbound too. Great generals, statesmen, personalities such as Sarah Bernhardt and various royalties were also under his sway, though one of his most devoted admirers, Carmen Sylva, Queen of Roumania, was herself a very accomplished poseur.

Loti was not only lionised by the public; he was adored by his friends to whom he became a cult, and to whom he showed a simpler side, a childish sense of fun. As to the extravagant manner in which he was lionised, it speaks for the place writers once held, that photographs of Loti sold in tens of thousands among all kinds of people. In Loti's day, to be a poet, a poetic writer, was *'la gloire'*. It was the romantic nineteenth-century conception of 'Literature', of literary demi-gods; the attitude which had fostered Byron, Pushkin, Victor Hugo and Lamartine.

Loti transposed exoticism from aristocratic flamboyance to a more bourgeois intimacy. It was in key with his age. The assassin's dagger had become bric-à-brac—the furnishings of a drawing-room. For Byron exoticism was a medium, a way to exalt and dramatise the tragedies of his characters. But with Loti, for the first time, exoticism became a quality on its own, and from a literary point of view, a whole subject. Victor Hugo, too, made use of exoticism, but in the Byronic-romantic manner: it was reserved for Loti to tame, or present exoticism for itself, the transposition being made by way of Gautier.

In the last decade of the nineteenth century, travel was still something remote from the general public, reserved for the rich, for commercial travellers, or the adventurers. Voyages were long and costly with unimaginable diseases lurking in every port of call. Even luggage told of the difficulties involved —gigantic iron-bound leather or tin trunks with domed lids, almost immovable even when empty, and requiring storage space which by today's standards would represent an extra room. No airlines or cars brought exotic horizons within reach for the annual holiday. It was still an age when most Europeans went, in July or August, to the nearest sea, and sat there, facing it, or dipping in it, until time to turn round and go home again. Their curiosity as to foreign parts remained ungratified. They attended lantern-slide lectures, or collected crudely coloured postcards. All travel, all far horizons were invested with mystery and romance. How strong, then, the spell that Loti's writings cast. He shared with his readers his own poetic sense of wonder confronted by these horizons, and his fervour was that of a lover discovering, and possessing in them, many different aspects of the beloved.

✧   ✧   ✧

In spite of the fame and fortune Loti's writings brought him, and in spite of that other dimension of dreams—that poet's limbo land in which he had his true being—nothing, no philosophy, no detachment could compensate for the gnawing knowledge that he was far too short-legged for the classic perfection he craved. In vain he was photographed in tights, in athletic poses with rippling, hard-won muscles; in uniforms blistered with equally well-won decorations, or in dashing Balkan costumes, staring out with his proud wounded stare. The fact remained—he was stumpy. Even as a child he disliked his appearance. 'I was not "my type",' he said. But perhaps his favourite device, *Mon Mal j'enchante*, with which he decorated his blue and gold dinner service, and inscribed in many of his books, explains the various costumes and disguises which were his weakness, and which, says Edmond de Goncourt, all claws out, made his life a perpetual carnival.

Loti tried to escape his limitations in other ways too: by means of high heels, and not always discreet touches of make-up; above all, muscular prowess, keeping himself at circus pitch with gymnastic feats. He was inordinately proud of having appeared in a circus act, genuinely admired by the professionals, and once alarmed Frank Harris by executing some dangerous backward somersaults in the course of a stroll through the garden of his friend, Princess Alice of Monaco. For many years the only means of entry to his study was by a swinging rope ladder up which he swarmed squirrel-like, enjoying, with that childish sense of fun, so oddly at variance with his morbidity, the frantic efforts of his less agile visitors who had hoped to see the master in his *cadre*.

Loti-land

Loti always worshipped physical strength: it was an expression of the eternal youth he craved, not so much for itself as for its denial of the final annihilation which was his horror. This note of dread sounds through all he wrote. He is obsessed by the ultimate darkness. Neither the Roman Catholic religion of his youth nor the Moslem faith for which he longed, could dispel this profound despair. Like love and youth, life could not endure. Irrevocably, all led towards a tragic finale. Every joy was overshadowed. Every kiss ended on a sigh; even in Aziyadé's arms he was quoting Oriental poetry: 'Each season draws me towards the night . . . O! Seigneur, to where do I go? And who will be beside me when I must drink that bitter cup?'

We still find this mood echoed in Istanbul, where Loti's *hélas!*, his *other times!* and *other places!* take positive form, overcoming the present. Graveyards abound: that other, still grey world of the Turkish cemetery is omnipresent, even now, among markets, beside cafés, and taxi-ranks, replacing the little parks and gardens of other cities. Slender-stemmed tombstones, each flowering into a turban, fez or garland, each turban carved with the fantastic windings and invention of its epoch, seems a stone bloom, a top-heavy tulip, flowering on, through the centuries, behind the grilled wall-windows that enclose these street graveyards. Peering through, we see rank grasses, knee high, where stray cats slink, stalking a bird, savaging a rag of greasy paper in which someone has thrown them a handful of scraps. Loti loved cats especially, and wrote of them as no one else but Colette has done. He suffered for all animals, as *Le Livre de la Pitié et de la Mort* bears anguished testimony.

Enmeshed in what was always, to him, the tragedy of life, Loti's principal distractions, after those meditative withdrawals which I have already mentioned, were found in music and dressing up—romantic disguises. In his cabin on board the various ships he came to command in his maturity, he would surround himself with a most un-nautical décor, Chinese porcelains, Persian brocades and rare prayer carpets. Here, beside cupboards filled with caftans and gandourahs and burnouses, he would sit at his piano for hours at a time playing Chopin—only Chopin. The pellucid phrases floated out across the water and along the shores of the Bosphorus to the *yalis*, or summer palaces, where, behind the moucharabias, many pairs of melting eyes were turned towards the ship. Loti was *coqueluche* of drawing-room and harem alike.

Shutting the piano with a sigh (Hélas! everything passed; even the afternoon was sliding irrevocably from his grasp) the Commandant would order the cutter to be brought alongside in half an hour; and opening the wardrobe he would select some fancy-dress outfit, by which he hoped to escape from reality into that exotic ambience he craved.

Wherever he went, Loti flung himself into the masquerade with an enthusiasm which was touchingly childish and quite at variance with his world-weariness. He plays his heroes with bravura, or pathos, as the rôle requires. He poses before the photographer's back-drop, Moroccan Loti in a burnous, in a gandourah, among the Senegalese, in Zouaves costume, living every page of *Le Roman d'un Spahi*, Loti with a fan beside Madame Chrysantème, though here he retains Western dress and a certain air of superior detachment; or, garlanded by caramel-skinned charmers, celebrating *Le Mariage de Loti*, a book which he illustrated himself with the same elegant facility with which he played the piano. *Le Roman d'un Spahi* first appeared with his haunting evocations of Senegal where the story is set. We see the shores of huge rivers, sands, broken only by a group of monstrous baobab trees or a solitary, crouching negress, beside the conical huts of a village stifled under a pall of leaden heat, and where the great birds of prey circle ceaselessly.

Loti's habit of adding an element of fiction, or ambiguity to his experiences, of placing a *moi* in every landscape, was summed-up by one critic who, in writing '*mais les mariages de*

Loti se font partout', could not avoid sounding a faint note
of envy, perhaps. But if Loti displayed a Don Juanistic
attitude towards many countries and their women, Turkey
(and Aziyadé) was his real love to which he remained
faithful.

Thus, above all the rest of the fancy dress, we see Loti the
Turcophil; he wears baggy trousers, a gold embroidered jacket,
and a fez. In the novel, Aziyadé's lover is a young English
naval officer. The *Deerhound* is anchored up the Bosphorus,
and at night, assuming Turkish dress, in which he has the grace
to admit he feels uncomfortably like an operatic tenor, the
English Lieutenant, who, rather bewilderingly, is still called
Loti, keeps a series of reckless rendez-vous with his mistress,
first in a gilded caïque massed with cushions, 'a floating bed',
and later, hidden away in the small house up the Golden Horn,
at Eyüb. But after a great deal of unnecessary suffering it all
ends badly. Fate separates them. Loti is ordered to sea. Aziyadé's
imprudence is discovered by her old master, and she is left to
pine and die. When Loti returns, it is, of course, too late.
Hélas and *Jadis*...! He quits the navy, joins the Turkish
forces, and dies in the flower of his youth, fighting for Turkish
independence.

When, twenty-five years later, Loti returned to Constantinople as a world-famous writer, he was Captain of his
ship, still a dashing figure, but the sun was sinking. He loved
his life on board and was adored by his crew, among whom was
the youthful Claude Farrère, whose life followed superficially
something of the same pattern—naval officer, exotic novelist
and Turcophil. Again the ship was anchored in the Bosphorus;
again a cutter brought Loti ashore. But now the cutter took
him less often towards adventure and the cut-throat alleys of
Tophane than towards the world of Pera and the embassies,
where, an adulated figure, he presently entangled himself in the
snares of three mischief-making women (one of them a French
journalist) posing as stifled victims of the harem. Loti, the

romantic revenant, going back on the elusive tracks of his youth, became their gullible victim. With touching eagerness he would tip-toe off to those clandestine meetings in the mysterious house behind Ahmedieh. When in *Les Désen-chantées* he described it all, he placed it elsewhere: but there is no mistaking that he saw himself as the hero, André Lhéry. The ladies led him on without scruple and when the whole ignoble affair was exposed, Loti's reputation suffered. The book is indifferent, and save for some beautiful descriptions of Stamboul, not worthy of the man who could write *Vers Ispahan.*

But this was only one episode of so many, acted out against the city which remains forever his. Truth and fiction, autobiography and posturing, all are interwoven. Haunting Loti! His power is such that there is no street, no aspect that does not conjure him.

Such is Loti's obsessive quality that however much we know he was, in his protracted Turkish farewells, really only taking an egoist's leave of his youthful hey-day, we still search out the scenes of his joys and sorrows, as if they were some historic site. We still go through the streets of Khassim Pacha recalling his description of a sunrise seen from the house where he first lodged, waiting for Aziyadé to rejoin him. 'Sketched in rose-coloured tints, a dome and its minarets emerged . . . little by little, the silhouette of the Turkish city appeared, as if suspended in the air . . .' And then, firmly placing himself in the landscape, 'And then I remembered that I was at Stamboul and that she had sworn to come there.' That was the rose-coloured morning. There are many other, more sombre evocations. Loti's lyricism could give place, at times, to dramatic effects as startling as a clap of thunder over the minarets; as in the terrible description of Fatou-Gaye finding the body of the Spahi: or the opening page of *Aẕiyadé*, where the hanged men kick and dangle along the waterfront of Salonika: or that dark note of passion sounding in a scene where Loti is telling his mistress of his love, and she seems not to be following:

'Aziyadé', I said, 'are you listening?'

'No', she replied. And then, in a low voice, at once gentle and savage: 'I would like to eat the sound of your voice.'

Such words must have quite taken the sting out of any suspected inattention, and been balm to any man, let alone such an egoist as Loti. 'Ah! Who will give me back my Eastern life?' he asks, again and again.

✤   ✤   ✤

In Istanbul, as in Loti's writing, there is the same thread of violence lying behind the beauty, something sensed rather than seen. This city is not facile. It does not offer itself at once. Its essence is uncomfortably uncompromising, and remains hidden from those who do not search for it. Above all, it is dramatic, and as such, it was irresistible to Pierre Loti. The quarter behind the Sülimanyé, or those vertical streets which go down towards the Seven Towers and the sea wall, are, before all else, sinister. The bleached, greyish wooden houses, with the windows of their top-heavy upper storeys sealed by close-grilled moucharabias seem to conceal dark secrets: we walk there, and are suddenly aware of a presence, observing us, a watcher, a shadow with eyes. This is the stealthy, forbidding city of which Gerard de Nerval wrote that it was like scenery, to be viewed from the front, without going behind. (Loti took us behind the scenes, but it was still theatre.) Nerval goes on: 'These painted houses, zinc domes and minarets are always charming to the poet, but 20,000 wooden houses so often visited by fire, the cemeteries where doves coo in the yew trees, yes, but where jackals dig up the dead when the great storms have loosened the soil . . . these are the reverse of the Byzantine medal.' Today, if the more picturesque aspects have faded behind the city's advancement, this Oriental mixture of the sinister, the beautiful and the sordid remains, the true Loti-land.

✤   ✤   ✤

To the Turkish people themselves, Loti is still a legend. They will talk to you of Sinans architecture, point out the delicate perfection of some street fountain, show you a radiance of blue tiles in some forgotten mosque; and with equal pride indicate a plaque on a particularly uninteresting-looking house in the Divanöglu where Loti lived. 'Have you been to Eyüp?' they ask, earnestly, as much on account of its association with him, as the fact that it is the holiest place in all Turkey, with sanctuaries no Christian may penetrate, the burial place of Eyüp Ansari, the Prophet's comrade and standard bearer.

We climbed the hills above its valley where the thousand pigeons strut and flutter in their chosen mosque, and where, half hidden in foliage, fragments of Turkish rococo gazebos and fountain courts lie beside the ornate *turbehs*, or sepulchres. They are remnants of an Imperial palace; today, even the fez-factory which was later established among its decaying splendours seems as remote as those Sultanate glories, vanished, along with the fez, along with the little house where Loti and his love dallied. But Loti's legend still lingers there. 'Loti . . . Loti café', said the vendor of the blue bead amulets and crude Koranic prints. He pointed to the scrubby hill top. 'Loti . . . To Loti?' asked the peasants we met on our way. They waved us on, up, pointing to the shack where, under straggling vines, some weather-beaten benches overlooked the windings of the Golden Horn, a panorama to silence all the guidebook rhapsodies. An old Turk sat there, smoking his tchibouk, contemplating the distant city, as Loti loved to do. The café proprietor lit a samovar and brought us the ritual glasses of tea. With the exquisite politeness of his race, he switched the radio from roaring Oriental moans to a Western station, equally insistent. The visitors, he inferred, would no doubt prefer European strains. He fiddled the knobs, and the machine screeched across a political agitator in Cairo, and a snatch of crooning, to settle into Chopin's Funeral March.

It could scarcely have been more appropriate, for most walks about Istanbul could be described as *marches funèbres*: outings have a curious way of centring round graveyards, or ending beside the sumptuous catafalques of some Imperial *turbeh*, which, however drawing-room in conception with crystal chandeliers, pearl-embroidered velvet hangings and carpets, is still a tomb. So many tombs, all echoing Loti's 'Never more!' By boat, or tram, or taxi, all roads lead to the grave: foxy old Barbarossa's tomb in the little park at Beşiktaş, where the children and nursemaids play among the lilacs: the Giant's Grave, Joshua's, they say, overlooking the inky expanses of the Black Sea: the tomb of Mahmoud II's favourite charger at Üsküdar, or Scutari, where everyone makes a pious pilgrimage to the Crimean War cemetery and the scene of Florence Nightingale's heroic labours. Tombs everywhere; on Fridays, the Moslem holy day, there are picnic outings to the cemeteries where, quietly, but cheerfully, the Turks sit beside their dead in confident communion, often bringing the departed's favourite food, for in the midst of life we are in death, and to the Turks, the dividing line is slight. In Loti's day, quick and dead were linked in even more aspects of pleasure. It was customary for prostitutes, at night, to flit about the cemeteries, where, having acquired a client, they would gratify him, there and then, on stony couches shadowed by the cypress and the yew.

Even now, on jolly bathing expeditions to the Princes Isles, someone is sure to point out the rock on which the Turks cast many thousands of stray dogs, bane of the streets, to die lingeringly, in Allah's own time—a more humanely organised end being contrary to Moslem tenets. A shadow falls on the picnic outing, and the dog-loving infidels try to think of other things . . . but once again, they have looked on death.

At Üsküdar, where efficient car-ferries now chug ceaselessly between Europe and Asia, the dominating impression still has this sombre quality. The cypress thickets rise steeply behind the town, to the most celebrated cemetery of all. 'Mighty death-field, PANORAMA,' says Murray's *Handbook* for 1892, which is the vintage I like my guidebooks to be. Besides, it is Loti's hey-day, and essentially, still applicable. Murray may remind us that Üsküdar derives from the Persian word for courier, or runner: that Üsküdar was the first station of the Asiatic couriers heading eastwards: that it was the assembly point of the great camel caravans heading towards Asia, to Bokhara, the Turcoman steppes—all Central Asia. We, less adventurous, may set out to follow the Bulbul Derisi, or Nightingales' path, but are, first of all, conscious of that dominating cemetery. Wherever we go in Istanbul, if we ask the way, we are certain to be told to keep the cemetery on our left, or our right, or to go past some 'little field of the Dead'. Everywhere, in the uproar, or in the stillness, the shades close in. We may go to the Sublime Porte in a tram, but it is the tram which seems unreal. Everywhere we are more aware of the dead than the quick; and Loti is always there, brooding among the steles with a dread of death, a repugnance, and yet a morbid fascination for graveyards, wholly at variance with the fatalistic Eastern beliefs he admired.

If melancholy inspired Loti's finest work, it seems that in Istanbul, too, sorrow and remorse have produced some of the loveliest expressions of Turkish architecture. The Shahzadeh mosque, for example, commemorates the unhappy princes Mulhammed and Jehangir, sons of Süleyman the Magnificent, who met their end through the machinations of their step-mother, Roxelane, determined on the advancement of her own son. The mosque of Mihrimah at Scutari tells of that day when, at its consecration, the populace rebuked the Sultan for his little son's arrogance towards them. On the instant the Sultan stabbed the child in public amendment for his omissions as a parent. The fatal dagger was walled up in the Prince's tomb, and its outline can still be seen along the marble side.

Tragedy, drama, decay, all three elements of the Turkish scene stimulated Loti. Could he have borne seeing the old thrust aside to make way for the progress so necessary to this race he loved? A welfare state would not have inspired him, I think, however much his sense of humanity might be in theoretic agreement. Sunset was better than sunrise; endings appealed more than beginnings. Eyes were more fascinating seen through a grille, over a yashmak. Aziyadé's tomb held him as perhaps her bed would not have done.

Except for the simplicity with which he writes of animals, Loti often sounds a thoroughly theatrical note; but then that is all part of his magic. It has something of the intoxicating unreality of grand opera. Although he liked to use his landscapes, his local colour, as backgrounds for his own pinings, to us, the readers, they always become foregrounds. Loti saw them as a framework in which he played out the perfect rôle—perfect from the masculine viewpoint, that is. He loves, and sails away before the problem of satiety arises. There are tears, and Loti's wonderful evocations gleam through them, sharpened by finality. These Circassian Kadines, these Serbian shepherd girls, these dusky beauties waving farewell from the Bosphorus, from a rooftop of the Kasbah or a tropic beach, it is always the same pattern of voluptuous partings, elegiac sorrows. Death or malign fate always overtakes them. Loti always sails away. 'Adieu' or 'Come back!' they cry. But he does not: cannot. And if he does, it is too late. '*Eúlú*! Dead!' the old negress Kadidja hurls at him, when he returns to search the quarter where Aziyadé lived, those grey, silent streets beside the Fatih which have not I think, changed much, since he wrote of them so beautifully. The wrenching farewells reach a last orgy of grief in *Suprêmes Visions d'Orient*, where, in spite of Loti now being accompanied by his grown-up son Samuel, the melancholy is quite overpowering.

All sorts of spiteful things have been written about Pierre Loti. He had his enemies, or rather his detractors, for someone of his largeness and essential goodness had few enemies. Aziyadé was said to have been no odalisque, escaped from the harem of a rich old Turk, but a prostitute, astutely presented to Loti in this more romantic guise. . . . She was said to have been a boy . . . she was said to have been a figment of Loti's imagination; but Loti himself was categoric in his denials. It had all happened as he wrote it: her name was Hakidjé: he would remember her until his last breath. In Farrère's description of Loti's end, it seems that he did. Even then, his sense of theatre prevailed. A dying man, he received his guests in the chill candle-lit dusk of the private mosque he had installed in his house at Rochfort, where Aziyadé's stelé reigned supreme.

✤   ✤   ✤

However much Loti dramatised, he had, too, a camera eye for verity. Some of his straight reporting, such as that on the Boxer Rebellion, has a steely impact. Even when romanticising, he never writes of places or ways of life he does not know well. Thus, he tells us little of the one place, above all others, of which he should have written—the Seraglio, or Vieux Sérail, fabulous palace of the Ottoman dynasty, at once fortress and prison which dominates the straits between Europe and Asia. Today, most of it (excepting the inner labyrinths of the sérail) is open to the public as a museum, filled with treasures beyond description. Its towers, domes, kiosques and outer bastions rise from the wooded slope of the lower gardens, now given over to an Amusement Park where, amid swings and roundabouts, sober Turkish families sit drinking tea and taking their pleasures rather austerely.

Loti-land

Another link, this, between Loti and the Turks. He too could be austere.

For all his exoticism he came from a severe northern French province: his family background was also strict. This northern quality is apparent to all who know the Turks beyond their superficially glowing Levantine legend. Turkey, it must be remembered, is not Mediterranean; it is a northern, Asiatic land where, sometimes, a southern sun blazes down; but, more often, the wind from the steppes howls wolfishly round. Loti loved best this chill aspect of Constantinople, and although his descriptions seem to glow with colour and light, they are, in fact, more often concerned with winter scenes: rain lashing across the landing stages; the livid skies of snow-storms; winter nights, winds moaning down the conical, hooded chimneys; rain beating down to foam through the refuse-piled gutters; damp mists closing in, muffling sight and sound. All these aspects of the city we find reflected in Loti's writing.

There are contradictions in both Loti and in the land. Opulence beside austerity. Take the Turkish passion for richness, seen in their palaces, their cuisine, jewellery and arts: Loti shared this love of the extravagant. But in his house at Rochfort, the home of his childhood (and it was part of his cult for the past that he kept the house, the old servants, his mother's room, all unchanged; a sort of hallowed temple of yesterday), he also allowed his flamboyance full rein. Here he amassed a varied collection of Eastern splendours, even to the acquisition of an entire mosque, transported stone by stone, from Damascus. It was of the Sunnite cult—red marble pillars and a gold-encrusted Mihrab, very splendid. Loti admitted he thought it the most beautiful mosque he had ever seen. Besides this, he had gratified his sense of theatre with vast renaissance halls, a mediaeval salon, Chinese and Japanese rooms, Turkish divans and Algerian alcoves, all placed behind the discreet façade of the original house and the neighbouring ones into which he had gradually spread, to accommodate his treasures.

It is eloquent of his tact, his respect for the old forms, that outwardly the little street remained untouched, sober Rochfortaise architecture.

Some aspects of the Seraglio, particularly its huggermugger of glories and ruin, would have been very much to his taste, and beneath the gilding lay tragedies which would have nourished him for years. Yet, it seems that he was never familiar with it. In his day, it was still Imperial property, though the Sultans had withdrawn, one by one, to other, less haunted palaces along the Bosphorus. While the Seraglio lay abandoned the Sultan Abdul Hamid II lived among his menagerie, his concubines and his fears, at Yildiz, or in the zebra-striped marbles of Tcheregan.

When, as often happened, Loti was shown some special marks of Imperial esteem and received by the Sultan, it was, unfortunately, always at some other, less historic palace, or at the Friday Selamlik, or levée, usually held in the sugar-cake décor of Dolmabagtché, 'not quite in the best of taste', according to the censorious Murray.

To the Turks whom he always championed, particularly in the dark hours of the Balkan wars, Loti had become a national figure. On his last visit, it was decided to bestow some exceptional favour upon him, and they found a graceful way to do it. A house near the Sultan Selim mosque, high above the Golden Horn, was furnished in the old Turkish manner with treasures from the Imperial palaces: rugs beyond price, embroideries, divans, jewelled tchibouks, all the settings of Loti's dreams. Here he was installed as the Sultan's guest. Servants from the palace dressed in their traditional costumes waited on the master, serving him and his friends with the rarest dishes. Nothing could have given him greater pleasure. No one could have been worthier of the compliment. Later it was regretted that he had not been offered a suite of rooms in the Seraglio. Its revenants? He, of all people, would have welcomed them, feeling himself one among them. Among its splendours and miseries he would have heard the pulse of the old Turkey he loved, and to which, today, we can still return, through his eyes.

Whatever else I have missed by the accident of having been born in the twentieth century, a hundred years too late for a person of my backward inclinations, I have, nevertheless, been able to know something of that old city which is the core of Loti-land. There is a Turkish saying, a farewell benediction, *Guleh*—go with a smile. They always say it to me, when I leave. But I always go with a sigh.

15

Laurence Hope—
A Shadow in the Sunlight

In the blaze of an Indian noon—the last brilliance of Imperial India—a shadow fell across that shimmering scene, merged with the dusk beneath the sinjib trees and was gone, leaving only a legend of some burning love, some perfume of the East, fugitive as a flute song, telling of lovers trysting on the roof tops of an ancient city, of floating enlaced on a lotustide; of raptures, revenge by cold steel, tears, sighs, then silence. This is Laurence Hope's legacy. Three small volumes of impassioned verse, a few scattered memories or letters from those who knew her; the reticence of her son, and a host of conjectures which sprang up round the charming, strange, withdrawn, yet forthright woman who, today, is only vaguely recalled as author of some exotic songs hackneyed by misuse.

The Indian Love Lyrics deserved a better fate. They were set to music by Amy Woodforde-Finden and for twenty years the palm courts of Grand Hotels and bric-à-brac-filled drawing-rooms rang with over-expressive renderings of these sensuous poems. 'Pale hands I loved, beside the Shalimar . . . whom do you lead on raptures roadway far?': so sang the sopranos and tenors, juicily, their accompanist, soft pedal down, swaying in matching fervour. 'I would rather have felt you round my throat, crushing out life, than waving me farewell!' . . . Loud pedal now, the singer, bosom arched and eyes closed, reaching for the last despairing note. . . . Tum tum ti ti tum tum ti went the accompanist accentuating the evocative Eastern rhythms, drowning the rattle of coffee cups. '. . . Less than the Dust beneath Thy Chariot Wheels' the cry of the despairing, adoring Eastern slave-wife was a particular favourite with brisk Anglo-Saxon ladies, until, at last, the beautiful and the violent world of India which Laurence Hope conjured, was forgotten, shouted down by jazz and more clinical expressions of love.

Would she have cared? I do not think so. She wrote organically, for herself, for love of love, of India, in an explosion of emotion, a process of internal combustion, even. It is contended that she could not have expressed such passions without living them, and when first her poems broke on an enthusiastic and titillated London public in 1901, and she was revealed, in spite of the pseudonym, to be a woman, gossip buzzed round her. Every line was construed autobiographically. She was that pretty, rather unconventional little Mrs. Nicolson? No, really! well, she simply couldn't have felt that way about her husband they said; he was twenty years older, a stern soldier. . . . Could he have inspired those sort of lines? All those descriptions of—well, of *love-making* . . . of such violent Oriental passions . . . so *very* frank. . . . No: it must have been some Indian prince, some sepia Romeo. That fitted much better. And then there was her sister, Victoria Cross, who wrote the most daring books, quite often about white women falling in love with Indians. Thus vulgar gossip. The Nicolsons remained an enigmatic pair: they were rarely in London, disliking the chill, petty horizons of civilization. They returned to India which was their whole life. Three years later both were dead.

✤   ✤   ✤

To the world Laurence Hope has remained a shade—curious fate for one so vital in both her life and writings. She has always interested me, and when I was writing *The Wilder Shores of Love* I wished to include her among my four biographies: but my research did not give me enough material.

Today I am a little better informed and much indebted to her son's unpublished memoir. But there are still many gaps, and no one left alive to fill them. Her son has been approached several times to collaborate on plays or films based on his mother's life: no doubt these would become exuberantly fictionalized, and so, abhorrent to him. 'But of course, the public do not want so much truth as a good story', he writes.

❧   ❧   ❧

Yet Laurence Hope's story is a wonderful one—even the little we know, being charged with colour, emotion, adventure and tragedy. Her setting was India—Kipling's India, part of that pattern of Empire-building in which England still believed: the India of might and right: of Viceregal splendours imposed on Moghul memories; of inequalities, yet idealisms, too, among the Indian civil servants and military caste with whom she lived, but from whom, in a sense, she was always apart.

I know of no other Englishwoman who penetrated India with the same sensuous understanding as Laurence Hope. Loving it she found, through it, many aspects of fulfilment which her ardent nature craved. It never seems to have occurred to those who analyse her verses, or those who ferret out other people's private lives, that emotions can be transposed to places, houses, things—above all, to countries. Many of Laurence Hope's most impassioned lines can be read in this light. In the blazing nimbus of the East she found the attributes of a beloved—mystery, beauty, cruelty, refinements of volupté and ancient wisdoms.... Before all else, I think she lived a love affair with a land, striving to possess it, knowing herself possessed.

Her verses, some inspired by legends of the people, by their literature, some from the depths of her own emotion, have left a portrait of this love in many guises. A lover to his mistress, a slave to her unattainable lord and master, an exile to his home; tender legends, terrible ones, the anguished cry of the deserted lover, the call of the prowling jackal at dusk ... and always, the scarlet thread of longing—of an atavism stronger than all else, the cry of a being trapped in the aeons of time, scenting, deep in the jungle, some kinship with the first stirrings of this land.

'O! life, I have taken you for my lover!' she wrote. But it was India which was, for her, the incarnation of her passion, the means by which she lived to the full, seeking to be one with the plains and the hills, the animals and the flowers; to know the many races, their beliefs and lives. Often she went among them secretly, living dangerously, beside her husband, in some frontier campaign: riding from battle into the stillness of the jungles, or the latticed world of the zenanas, listening to tales of love and jealousy. *The Regret of the Ranee in the Hall of the Peacocks, Yasin Khan, The Lament of Yasmini the Dancing Girl*, or *The Rao of Ilore* are all culled from the people, while she went among them as a woman, as a man (disguised as a Pathan boy), as a European, as an Indian, but always coming closer to the beloved.

'Heart, my heart, thou hast found thy home!' is the opening line of her *Song of the Parao*, something far more likely to be autobiographical than many others held to be so revealing.

> These are my people, and this is my land
> I hear the pulse of her secret soul ...
> ... Washed in the light of a clear fierce sun,
> Heart, my heart, the journey is done.

Over and over she sounds this ecstatic note: in her writings as in her life she was identified with the East as few Europeans dared or cared to be. Especially women. In India at that time, Englishwomen held to a code as rigid as any caste system. The memsahibs of Poonah and Simla or the plains grew fretful drilling legions of bewildered native servants to recreate the conventions of Kensington or some country town they had enshrined. For them, India was exile. They remained un-initiated, playing bridge, planting sweet-peas or delphiniums in preference to the heady blossoms of the tropics, the moghra flowers, the champa and the lotus which Laurence Hope loved. *Under the Deodar* was a popular song: at the club-house dances they valsed to it, while sighing for northern beeches, and felt themselves unquestionably more attractive than the undulating Nautch girls who were said to offer competition, down in the bazaars.

For women, then, India remained something which, even if it began to charm them must be kept at arm's length, like some dangerous seductor.

Not for the memsahibs the romantic old Bari-dari, or garden houses, set in mango groves, with marble floors, fretted pillars and mirrored gilded ceilings, cooled by fountains and water-courses. They preferred gabled bungalows with chintzy drawing-rooms and roast-meat menus. Their lives were lived behind ramparts of nostalgia. Few, very few of the women, at that time, who were truly interested in India. Flora Annie Steele, and Maud Diver, in their own way; but it was not Laurence Hope's way.

'If anyone was cabined, cribbed and confined by circum-stances, it was she,' wrote Flora Annie Steele, the novelist and social worker, who lived half her life in India, and knew Laurence Hope briefly, as the bride of an old friend. 'Like some tropical bird, she was ensnared in the cage of civilization.' Mrs. Steele described her as 'a small athletic figure in bright-coloured satins. . . . A childlike face, a pair of wide blue eyes, not by any means unfathomable—they were far too clear for that—but full to the brim of eager curiosity, keen appreciation and unswerving directness.'

Another friend described her as 'riveting attention'. She had intensely blue eyes of a peculiarly deep, violet tint, so that her husband always called her Violet. Her build was slight—so narrow (in that wide-hipped age) that she looked like a schoolboy. She did not follow the fashion for piled up, frizzed up hair, but wore hers unconventionally, cut loose on her neck, framing her face, in the manner of a Florentine page. The few photographs I have been able to see reveal a strong rather brooding face, which could no doubt become beautiful in animation, and colour, but which in repose, and black and white, has a quality of wilful determination: the face of a woman who knew what she wanted, sought for it, fought for it, but who knew, too, how to yield: the face of a passionate woman.

✢   ✢   ✢

What was her background? Adela Florence Cory was born on April 9, 1865, at Stoke House, Stoke Bishop, in Gloucestershire. Her father, Arthur Cory, was a colonel in the Indian Army. Her mother, Fanny Elizabeth Griffen, was singularly lovely, of Irish descent. The family travelled much and Adela Florence and her two sisters spent their time between European cities and a private school in London acquiring the accomplishments then encouraged. Adela Florence was greatly gifted, was musical, composed, played and sang and painted with considerable talent. In the studios and salons of Florence, her artistic development matured precociously, and she is said to have written many verses at this time, though none are included in her collected works. When her parents returned to India, she was marooned in England, to complete her schooling. She seems to have been anguished by the separation: already she was a prey to the force of her emotions.

She was just sixteen when she joined her parents in India, but she was a mature and much-travelled young woman. At Lahore, her father edited the *Civil and Military Gazette*, and she began to work beside him. When he fell ill she took over, acquiring journalistic experience, even from so rigid a medium; for it is not to be supposed that this mouthpiece of the British Raj concerned itself with much beyond the perimeter of

Government House and the cantonments. (Kipling, however, as a young journalist of eighteen, worked as assistant editor on this same paper.) There is no record of her having written any verses at this time and her life appears to have been chiefly according to pattern, surrounded by the conventions of her kind, dancing, tennis, flirting ... but beginning to look about her with those wide and candid eyes, and to see another world, infinitely strange and compelling, forever removed from her own.

'And never the twain shall meet' wrote Kipling whose brilliance was proving most disturbing. While vaunting England's might, he also poured out his spleen on a certain type of Englishwomen in India. But *The Jungle Book*, like some other tales, proved his deep understanding of the country. Beyond the Cory's bungalow lay all that unattainable magic: the musky fragrance of the bazaars, with the opium dealers, grotesque toys and brilliant silks; the clay-daubed fakirs, the painted provocations of the dancing girls, the princely youths, dicing and quail-fighting, their scarlet and orange turbans mounted with jewels; and at dusk, the spangled notes of the *sita* floating out across the temples where the carvings of god-like lovers interlocked in eternal ecstasies. ... But none of this must ever be for the young Misses Cory.

For men, it was different. They could turn inward on native life for their pleasures; tiger hunts and polo with the Maharajahs, feasting in their marble palaces: learning something of the mystic-erotic cults of love in the arms of an amber-limbed girl. These men had chances denied to their womenfolk. They worked hard, and played hard, learning much about the land they had taken, esteeming its many races and creeds. Still, they generally married some pink-faced miss fresh from home, and forgot their flower-crowned nights, while their command of the different dialects rusted. But they had glimpsed that other world, and they were never quite the same again. Some echo, or longing, remained.

And what if a woman became aware of the virile beauty of Indian men? These descendants of Akbar and Jehangir? The proud Rajput warriors or a young tribesman glimpsed coming down from the wild hills? 'He trod the ling like a buck in spring and looked like a lance at rest,' wrote Kipling. The Pathans were reputed to be the most vicious and bloodthirsty, but their towering, godlike forms were considered the embodiment of Eastern beauty. These must have been disturbing thoughts for the impressionable, indeed, inflammable Adela Florence and her sister Vivian who, writing later as Victoria Cross, was to enlarge on this theme, as on inter-racial loves with obsessional force. She is particularly bitter on the subject of English intolerance. Christine is kidnapped by an Arab Sheik, and horrifies her friends by submitting: Hamilton pays 2000 rupees for a beautiful dancing girl who is murdered: Stanhope is in love with 'the Pearl of the Desert' who is stabbed. Trevor is desperately involved with Suzee, a Chinese girl. Frances, a General's daughter is discovered, in her bedroom, in the arms of a Pathan; the General knocks him out, but the lovers escape, to live in a native village. Of course, it all ends badly; intolerance all round. But we are left in no doubts as to the sentiments of the author.

I know nothing of Victoria Cross's personal life: I am not assuming her books to be autobiographical, any more than the poems of her sister Laurence Hope, but both are evidence that each woman, in her own way, was awake to the sensuous spell of the tropics, and had few conventional prejudices. One passage in *Anna Lombard* is noteworthy. It was Victoria Cross's most sensational novel, sold 250,000 copies and went into seventy editions, and was considered outrageous. In it, she described a martial dance of the Pathans, performed at Government House, before an Anglo-Saxon audience, among them, the heroine who, while sitting beside her long-suffering English fiancé, is secretly married to one of the Pathans, and has come to see her husband dance his barbaric dance of triumph there below, 'each dark face between a sword and a sword'. 'It was a sensuously beautiful sight, and as such sights are generally rendered by women for the benefit (or otherwise) of men', she goes on to describe its impact on the white ladies, who sat nervously fanning themselves, shivering with desire. 'A woman whose eyes had once been opened so that she could see that beauty, one whose senses were captured by it would never be free, entirely free, till death released her.'

This was strong meat, and although only published in 1901, there is no doubt it derived from the force of the author's youthful impressions, probably shared with her sister. There is no doubt, either that the young Misses Cory must have kept their thoughts to themselves. But *their* eyes had been opened, and they would always seek for something wild and free, beyond the cage of civilization.

For Adela Florence the next few years must have dragged. None of the many men she met appear to have interested her. Humdrum marriage with a pukkah-sahib was not for one who sought the pulse of adventure, and for whom India remained tantalizingly at arm's length.

But in 1889 the pattern changed. She met Colonel Malcolm Hassels Nicolson of the Bengal Army. He was a most remarkable man, and she must have recognized this at once. He was surrounded by an aura of daring and strangeness. Here is how one of his officers described him: 'Of splendid build, with a face once seen never forgotten, he at once impressed you as a man absolutely without fear of anything. He had spent his days soldiering among the wild tribesmen beyond Scinde; he knew their language and customs and had imbibed their spirit. But for his colour and Saxon tongue you might easily have mistaken him for a Pathan, when he made up his mind to turn out as one of that fine race. Possessing many peculiar ideas and caring not a jot who did or did not agree with them . . . he was at once a man you would follow anywhere, and a friend who went about seeking whom he might help in trouble.'

This then was the *preux chevalier* who was to prove, for Laurence Hope, the bridge by which she reached India; the man by whom she was, literally, swept off her feet. It was a curious episode. He was leaving for some remote destination, she was at the station seeing him off. The door of his compartment swung open and she was dragged along beside the train. Nicolson managed to pull her up to safety beside him. And so, brought together in the most unlikely manner, they remained together: we imagine them, the stern-faced, adventurous soldier of forty-six and the romantic, adventure-hungry girl of twenty-four, speeding forward into the torrid Indian landscape.

It was a happy marriage. Like had met like: he was the link between her inescapable Western roots and that atavistic urge which was her torment and delight. Their first years together were, for her, of ever-widening horizons. She had found a man who loved India and knew it as she longed to do. In her he found a companionship and daring not encountered in other women.

Malcolm Nicolson was of that special breed of nineteenth-century Englishman at once unconventional and traditional whose legend recurs in the annals of the British army: particularly in the East. Some were ascetics, military mystics, some were eccentrics; all were men of stern purpose, however exotic their preferences, and all knew the East intimately. I am reminded of Colonel Charles James Roberts, who raised the Bengal Lancers, married an Afghan Princess, and rallied many intractable tribes to his standard. He lived in style, with Nautch music for the Princess, and four hundred Rampuri hounds which were massaged daily with sweet-smelling oils. He wore a Kabul turban and his long dark locks falling on his shoulders, and administered justice from a fine rug set before his door, carrying a large handkerchief and a club, to weep with the afflicted or castigate the erring, as he saw fit. Such figures became legendary, 'living the East' dangerously, incorruptibly, in battle, in disguise, but ever loyal to their country; and it

must have been intoxicating to one of Laurence Hope's nature
to find herself allied to these traditions. Her husband was a
brilliant Oriental linguist, speaking Baluchi, Brahmi, Persian,
Pushtu and many more. His facility was probably acquired in
the classic manner of his kind, among the people, learning love
and languages together. Men with this background of adventure could never be dull, and it is astonishing that anyone could
have ever imagined Laurence Hope found life with her husband
such.

Malcolm Nicolson was born in 1843 of Highland Scottish
descent, his father before him, in the Bengal Army. He saw
much active service, in Abyssinia, at the capture of Magdala,
in the Afghan wars, and was covered in glory and medals.
Tales of his daring were many in the frontier regions and
Afghanistan, which he reconnoitred, disguised as a Pathan. As
a young man it is recorded that he crossed the tanks of Magapir
leaping barefooted from back to back of the sacred man-eating
crocodiles. This exploit, while much admired by his fellow
subalterns, has a ring of bravado, but as Gide says: we can
never be blasé over crocodiles. Evidently, Nicolson was a man
of supreme courage and his wife must have found this as
irresistible as the adventures—the campaigns, even, which she
now contrived to savour, at his side.

In the autumn of 1890 Nicolson was second-in-command of
the Zhob Valley expedition and she followed him, disguised as
a Pathan boy, creeping under his tent at night, following the
column on the march, spying out the land, crouching beside
him in battle, and by the camp fire. According to her son, to
whom I am indebted for much material: 'probably no woman,
outside a novel, has lived so adventurously in peace time'. But
was there ever peace in the N.W. frontier regions? Lone,
dangerous rides through tribal country, to wild trysting places,
in those angry passes; in her own words 'the sky tent-like
above us, upheld by jagged peaks'. All the pace and danger of
those moments sound in her lines *To the Hills*:

> 'Tis eight miles out and eight miles in,
> Just at the break of morn
> 'Tis ice without and flame within,
> To gain a kiss at dawn. . . .

Or again, in *Yasin Khan*:

> Did we not waken, one despairing dawn
> Attacked in front, cut off in rear by snow
> Till, like a tiger leaping on a fawn
> Half of the hill crashed down upon the foe . . .

and later

> . . . the red tears falling from thy shattered wrist
> A spent Waziri, forceful still in hate
> Covered thy heart ten paces off—and missed.

Jingle, if you like, but how intoxicating to have lived!

Now her blood was up: she could not relinquish such a life. She studied various dialects, travelled about the country widely, and luxuriated in her new freedoms. Sometimes the Nicolsons vanished, on long, solitary frontier reconnaissances which were known and valued by the Government. Later, for her, there were more and more excursions into native life. Dangerous, hidden excursions into various temple initiations and secret rites—cults which were little known among the Indians themselves, rites which took place in temples carved in the rock, or in caves deep in the jungle. She was believed to be the only European woman—perhaps the only European of either sex who was an initiate of the Taubuk mysteries. Few dared to approach them, but life in all its aspects, all of that India she loved so profoundly were sought by Laurence Hope. Her curiosity was vigorous, childlike, never prurient. 'Evil slipped from her', wrote a friend. She wanted to know—to live—to know all of that stream of life into which she plunged with such eagerness. Mysteries, countries, people.

Not that she welcomed bores. One caller described petulantly how 'she pretended to be asleep when I called. But I noticed she woke up at once when Major Willcocks came in.'

She followed her husband on all his different appointments, preferring the camp life to that of a big station; there she was apt to be regarded as unorthodox. Mrs. Steele, recalling a meeting in Bombay, wrote of her embarrassment, sitting beside this striking figure, 'dressed in a low-necked, short-sleeved pink satin gown, in an open victoria in broad daylight. It seemed a pity, with all those dark eyes looking on, and British prestige looming in the distance.' But she went on to say they were a very happy pair who outweighed thousands in brains and brilliancy.

It was a corseted age, and when Laurence Hope received her visitors reclining on a sofa, with bare feet, her hair hanging down her back, she shocked them. Even her sense of humour was mistrusted. Changing clothes with a youthful A.D.C. and driving round the station together was severely condemned by all but the junior officers and her husband, who always understood and indulged her.

Gradually, the life of adventure which the Nicolsons valued became more and more curtailed by his promotions. In 1894, as Major General and C.B., he was in command of a most important cantonment—Mhow. And now, as once they had ridden dangerously together into the frontier zones, they assumed the responsibilities of this position and the wearing round of official entertaining. Their house had been a small Rajah's palace; they preferred it to the military headquarters provided and here they received with great elegance—beautiful old silver, fine wines and food and a lavish, almost Oriental massing of tropical blossoms. In spite of a marked reserve which always hedged them, they were very popular: their team-work was perfect and they were truly interested in every aspect of their post. Sometimes she would lecture the young soldiers, and they would listen meekly: she was so disarming, so delightful, so unlike any other woman, they said, and made her their confidante, trusting her, as did the Indian peoples who sensed her sympathy for them.

Mhow was set in the Great Central Indian plateau, ringed by

the Vindhya mountains: a savage and beautiful face of India, and a bastion of the British Raj, placed there to subdue any recurring trouble with the turbulent Holkars. The Union Jack fluttered on the ramparts and the guns boomed their salvoes to mark the comings and goings of the Commander. Those of his wife were scarcely less remarked, for they were surrounded by an aura of daring. No other woman ever even wanted to go, as she did, alone into the hills and jungles, absenting herself for days at a time, apparently to study strange rites, temples, or some new dialect. To paint too: curiously quiet, meticulous work, faithfully recording the lovely country around her, 'which, as her art matured made very acceptable gifts', notes her son primly. Even so, her underlying sense of tragedy and drama is apparent. In one, beneath the palms, lies the naked body of a murdered native cradled in a dark stain of blood.

About now, she began to admit, diffidently, that she wrote poems: sometimes she gave them to her friends, or they appeared in local club journals: but always anonymously. It was prudent: some of her subjects would have caused eyebrows to have been raised to disappearing point in the curled bangs worn by the other English ladies. Poems such as *The Night of Shiva*, would have been considered far too outspoken by polite society then, lines about places, climates, landscapes . . . they were admirable—to be quoted—'jagged mountains that gnaw against the hard blue Afghan sky . . .'. But what about the fate of the wanton whose 'body lay with hacked-off breasts, dishonoured in the pass . . .'. Or that *extraordinary* poem called *Afridi Love* . . .

> When I have slowly drawn my knife across you
> Taking my pleasure as I see you swoon . . .

or that other:

> Paler and paler grow my lips
> And still thou bids't them bleed.

Her husband explained away her verses laconically: 'My wife had quite a knack of expressing deep emotion and certain phases of native life,' he remarked to a friend, which gives the lie to those who later insisted he knew nothing of her poems, and that on discovering they were engendered by her violent love affair with an Indian prince, he took to his bed and died soon afterwards.

In 1891, on long leave from India, the Nicolsons embarked on a disastrous venture, putting £4000, a large sum in those days, into a scheme by which, with Sir John Lister Kaye, they would obtain railway, mining and river-navigation concessions in China. After some months of travel in the Far East, fighting to establish themselves in competition with various international syndicates they were forced to admit defeat. Still, there had been months of travel across China, and meetings with the inhabitants of the Forbidden City. From her poem *Wind o' the Waste On the Wall of Pekin*, we see how, once again the poetess could capture, in a few lines, the *genus loci*, the spirit, or essence of a landscape. It is a strange, cruel poem, matching the scene, and the episode recounted. It proves, like her poem *Rutland Gate*, or *Trees of Wharncliffe House*, both inspired by England, how exactly she could convey a climate, or the mood a country aroused in her.

Their return to Mhow in 1899 was joyous: they had come home. Here was the fiery heart of all the fiery kingdoms of India, rich things growing richly, jungles edging down to lakes; nearby the ruined city of Mandu, the red sandstone and marble masterpieces of Pathan architecture choked by vegetation: tombs, domed bath-houses, and groves of orange-coloured lantana, where, close by, the tigers burned as bright.

Mhow was not only a military centre: it was also the focal point of official life, and made more spectacular by the numbers of Indian princes who gathered there for the polo matches, and the hunting. There were the maharajahs and raos, and their courtiers; hereditary rulers, such as the Maharajadhiraja Maharana of Jaipur—royal of the royal; his costume 'a living map of emeralds', his heron tufted turban swagged with

colossal diamonds. His white marble palace rose from a vast
lake, and was ornamented by huge cut crystals, glittering in
the sunlight like a thousand more jewels. In their palaces, their
lives, their clothes and their proud and beautiful features, these
princes were fabled beings, living still in that feudal state which
civilization and the West threatened. As a woman, Laurence
Hope must have found them seduction itself. As a thinker, she
has left us a poem which speaks of her disgust for much of the
West—her own race, holding India in subjection.

> Though many things and mighty
> Are furthered in the West,
> The ancient Peace has vanished
> Before today's unrest . . .
> For how among the striving,
> Their gold, their lust, their drink,
> Shall men find time for dreaming
> Or any space to think?

For all its former military might, Mhow is remembered
for being 'the place where Laurence Hope wrote her hectic
verses' says a traveller visiting the place in 1929. 'The secretary
of the Maharajah [of Indore?] has reminiscences of her and how
her girlish marriage to an elderly man exemplified Hindu
ideas on the subject, that marriage is of the spirit and not of the
flesh.' Yet whatever, or whoever, fired Laurence Hope's
verses from Mhow, they still echo. The captains and the
kings depart, the temples crumble and the jungles invade: but
the pen is still mightier than the sword.

In the London Library, I found a vellum-covered edition of
The Indian Love Lyrics, inscribed 'from the Library of H.M.
Queen Mary'. The Queen, as Empress of India had made a
State visit there for the Delhi Durbar of 1911 and cherished
memories of that time. I like to think of this great Queen,
surrounded by her jade and Fabergé *bibelots*, in the sober
magnificence of the palace, evoking, through Laurence Hope's
ecstasies, those glowing horizons she had barely glimpsed.

Shadow in the Sunlight

Who can tell what sparks a writer—particularly a poet? The stimuli are many. Love, hate, boredom, penury.... Confronted by the question of what, or who, inspired Laurence Hope's descriptions of love and longing, which, if we assume they had to be inspired by experience, do not tally with some aspects of her life—then it is obviously easier to assume she lived some illicit affair with an Indian lover, for all the implications are there: snatched meetings, secrecy, young love, wild pulses, renunciations, regrets, longings, love, the act of love, even, as in *The Night of Shiva*, or, irrefutable proof to some, the poem *On the City Wall*.

> Upon the City Ramparts, lit by the sunset gleam,
> The Blue eyes that conquer meet the Darker eyes that dream ...

Yet we do not know. Were this love between the wife of the British commander and one of the princely Indian rulers to have flamed up, it is certain that the scandal would have been quickly stilled; both races would have seen it as unthinkable—a loss of prestige.

Thus, the mainspring of Laurence Hope's verses still elude us. She was a free soul, true to her own beliefs, who loved her husband deeply. Yet, if she, the younger by twenty years, was swept into some maelstrom of emotion and scandal, involving the clash of East and West, it is her husband of all people to whom she could have turned, who would have understood. It would have been part of that pattern of coming closer to the India they both loved. I do not infer anything so banal as a *mari complaisant*; such a phrase smacks of the facile manners of eighteenth-century France, held to be so authoritative on *l'amour*. Love, as the Nicolsons knew it, was of a very different calibre.

In the dedication of her last posthumous poems addressed to her husband, she writes:

> Small joy was I to thee: before we met
> Sorrow had left thee all too sad to save ...

And in a letter, referring to their last year together: 'he said he only wished he had known before how happy life could be . . .'.

What was this gnawing sadness? Why had sorrow marked him, before they met? Perhaps, long ago, he too had lived some tragic folly? In those days, young soldiers of his mettle put their private lives aside. 'Passion blazed in them and was harnessed to work and bodily vigour. A man who wished for marriage before middle-age was frowned on: it was an infidelity to the ideal of work', writes Philip Woodruff in *The Men Who Ruled India*. Perhaps, alone in knowing his story, his wife was sometimes voicing his griefs, too, in her verses?

A biographer's work is always a combination of detection and intuition: if the writer is attuned to the subject there is sometimes a kind of subconscious enlightenment, or communication. This is an experience common to most serious biographers. After the discipline of facts and the triumphs of discovery comes that flash of intuition, of awareness. Studying Laurence Hope with the few facts at my disposal I am of the impression that there was no flesh-and-blood lover—that India, and perhaps some unattained, forbidden passion sparked her already extravagant temperament to produce such fervent verses—and so, send the scandalmongers off on a false trail.

Sometimes, puzzled by the inconsistencies of a character, or by conjecture, convictions, even, which do not seem to tally with facts, I have turned to astrology for clarification. The East has always regarded the casting of horoscopes as an exact science. In the India of tradition, and even today, few marriages are considered suitable unless the horoscope of bride and bridegroom, and the chosen day are all propitious. In the case of Laurence Hope, being unable to obtain the precise hour of birth, only a *Speculative* Chart could be made. Having insufficient data the astrologer assumed the birth-hour to be after sunset, since this fitted the known facts of the life. Marriage, writing success, elements of secrecy, violent emotions and suicide were all indicated on a chart thus timed. Even with so imperfect a chart the analysis is remarkable. Her character appears to have been violently emotional, loyal, devoted, extravagant, with a very strong sense of justice and also of unconventionality and daring. The urge for unconventionality in many forms is shown by Uranus, placed so that the emphasis is especially connected with the sex life. There are added elements of danger, rashness and drama. But more benign aspect of Uranus and the Sun indicate that much of this turbulence was harnessed otherwise—in creative work.

'A strong, clear horoscope,' notes the astrologer, Mrs. Lind. 'Planetary forces are without ambiguity. Sun in its exaltation (Aries), Venus in its own sign of Taurus, Jupiter in its own sign of Sagittarius, Saturn in its exultation (Libra). Such a subject goes to extremes, with conviction.' I will only add, here, that in 1895, she appears to reach a climax of extravagant emotions: and in 1896–7, this force continues, stimulating creative forces, adventure, illusion, and the secret or sensational, that 1901 was a peak year, that from 1902 on, renunciation, and a decline are indicated. In her last year, 1904, where renunciation and sadness gather, Neptune transits Mars, a sinister implication for her, with a natal Mars Neptune square: this links sex and death, and stimulates her strong potential for emotional suffering, despair, tragedy, and self-destruction. Add to this Sun quincunx Saturn, in 1904—the classic aspect for death. Again, natally, she has the Sun opposite Saturn, which touches off this karma. In this year, all the tragic aspects of her stars, as of her life, combined.

I have been told fantastic stories (as fantastic, some readers will say, as my claim for the verity of a horoscope) concerning Laurence Hope's idyll with a Hindu prince: the whole episode ready-made for Hollywood: how they met at Mhow, and lived a brief and burning love, in secrecy and danger, meeting on the lotus lakes, or in the shade of the temples, she disguised as a dancing girl, he as a commoner, their pulses beating to the rhythm of the drums . . . of how the infatuated Prince vowed half his wealth and kingdom to her first-born . . . how the parchment deed was snatched, at some ceremonial scene, swallowed by a fanatic, or burned by another . . . how the Prince's father tore the lovers apart; how the Viceroy himself stepped in to hush up the scandal, how the Maharajah was compelled to abdicate. Perhaps this farrago all fits very neatly, but I am not convinced. Perhaps she loved—enough to precipitate scandal—but not enough to hurt her husband. Who knows, now? The bombshell quality of Laurence Hope's poems alone was enough to engender the wildest rumours.

In his *Writer's Notebook*, Somerset Maugham makes a reference to the affair as London interpreted it in 1901, the year *The Garden of Kama* first appeared. 'They were talking about V.F. (Violet Florence) whom they'd all known. She published a volume of passionate love poems obviously not addressed to her husband. It made them laugh to think that she'd carried on a long affair under his nose and they'd have given anything to know what he felt when at last he read them.'

Yes, I expect such people would have enjoyed such a situation. Maugham adds: 'This note gave me the idea for a story which I wrote forty years later. It is called *The Colonel's Lady*.' But when, the other day, I asked him if he could recall anything of Laurence Hope, or the incident, he replied that he was now in his ninetieth year, and had forgotten so much. In his same *Notebook*, he writes: 'how often the author makes up his fiction from incidents of his own experience, *trifling*, perhaps, *and made interesting or dramatic only by his power of creation*'. The italics are mine. Laurence Hope's powers of identification, of creative imagination were great. Did she need more?

High passions belong to all ages, all races, but it is the English, for all their seeming reserve, who display in their literature the most ardent emotions, the most lyric tenderness, and the most profound understanding of love in all its aspects.

Consider the dark face of love as Emily Brontë showed us, in *Wuthering Heights*: the love, at once metaphysical and sensuous, of which John Donne wrote; the heartbreaking desires of Shakespeare's sonnets; or that anonymous fifteenth-century lover whose verse still echoes the cry of every longing lover:

> O Western wind, when wilt thou blow
> That the small rain down can rain.
> Christ, that my love were in my arms
> And I in my bed again!

Here is that same stark note, that same abandonment to love which we find in the Scottish Border Ballads: And which we find in the poems of Laurence Hope.

Not that I am comparing her to the immortals. Still, her voice still vibrates; she still speaks to us of love, and we still listen.

✤   ✤   ✤

After the whispers of scandal, the fanfares of acclaim. When the General's term of office at Mhow was over, in 1900, their long leave began by a sojourn in Bombay where their only child, Malcolm Josceline, was born in September. Doctors despaired of the mother's life, and at this moment we have a clue to the depth of the bond between husband and wife, of some suicide pact even, which later, she was to honour. In a letter to an old friend, the General wrote that he had burned all his papers, and meant to follow her, as he had promised. Perhaps her excursions into the mystic cults of India had convinced them of some unity, after death.

But she recovered, and back in London, this world pressed in on them. All its conventions stifled them. When in 1901 Heinemann published her *Garden of Kama*, the acclaim was instant. Mr. Hope, an unknown young poet—for of course he must be young—showed a fresh and splendid talent. Critics and public wanted more. Then the secret leaked out. It was a

woman—Major-General Nicolson's wife! Now they found
themselves social lions, objects of curiosity and admiration.
But financial problems beset them. His leave was indefinite,
his next appointment uncertain, although he was still on the
active list, a Commander of the Bath, at Court Levées and the
Cavalry Club, where appointments are usually sealed.

Forgetting the lesson of their abortive Chinese venture, they
now considered tea-planting in Assam, or some lucrative post
in Morocco, where they went in 1902. In the great silences
of the desert and the sun, the exiles found something of their
own climate again. But French-held interests were too powerful for the establishment of any worthwhile venture: once
again they were defeated and returned to London. 1903 saw
the publication of *Stars of the Desert*; and a disastrous venture,
a newspaper, which Laurence Hope wished to run on new,
experimental lines. Their whole life was India: away from its
fiery shores they were lost. Her poems are not dated, but we
can place some precisely. *Trees of Wharncliffe House* is the song
of an exile:

> ... your leaves, refreshed by summer showers
> Are naught to me, who feast
> My fancy on those other flowers
> that burn about the East.

... and again:

> I always feel a sense of loss
> If, at the close of day
> I cannot see the Southern Cross
> Break through the gathered grey ...

So, in 1904, they returned to India, to await the expected
appointment. Leaving their child with the General's sister, they
sailed east once more, towards the sunlight. But for them, it
was setting, though its rays still warmed them as they wandered
from one modest hotel to another (no wild sorties, now, into
the frontier passes). A muted note of acceptance sounds in her
letters: the rebel has come to terms with life: she loves and is

loved, but both of them have known another pulse. She is thirty-nine, he is sixty-two.

> Ah! to exchange this wealth of idle days
> For one cold reckless night of Khorasan!

are lines which voice their sadness as the years closed round, imprisoning them.

They found life cheap in an Indian backwater. Necessities were few. They no longer entertained officially and so could live modestly. Her songs were sold for sums which, by today's values, seem insulting. Five guineas for one; three for another. Yet she was pleased. How few her demands on life, now.

She wrote home asking for pictures of her baby son, and showed, again, how modest her attitude to life. Penny snapshots by a beach photographer, she wrote, were often the best. They could be taken often, every day even, and could catch the subject perfectly. Like many passionate women she was not, I think, predominantly maternal: her husband came first. We imagine the lonely little boy, patting at sand castles, in charge of elderly relatives, sent home so early, staying behind when his parents returned to India; loved, but perhaps coming so late into their lives, not having time to become part of it before they died, leaving him forever a stranger.

For some while, the General had not seemed well. Not ill, but not the iron-constitutioned soldier with whom she had shared so much adventure. Suddenly, a chill wind of premonition stirs in the palms. The sun has lost its warmth. In Madras, the General's ill-health was diagnosed as trifling; a minor operation would set everything right. It would be better to have it done at once, before the awaited appointment was confirmed. Arm-in-arm they walked round to the nursing home. There was no cause for anxiety and they parted lightly. Next day, August 7, he was dead. He had been given too much anaesthetic, and then suddenly, there was not enough oxygen to revive him. It was a question of time. Frantically, the nurses and doctors tried to keep him breathing. Desperately Laurence Hope rushed from chemist to hospital in a bid for her husband's life. Oxygen cylinders could not be had. When she got back to the nursing home, living a nightmare from which she never again escaped, it was too late. Death had found Malcolm Nicolson, not as he would have wished, in battle, or in the hills, but in the inefficiency of a small nursing home.

For Laurence Hope, there was never any more sunlight: she had entered a twilight zone of grief. Her letters home were heartbreaking: she could not reconcile herself to her loss. She saw her husband everywhere: he was beside her—he was gone: sleeping, waking, she was possessed by sorrow. They had grown even closer, in these past few years of inactivity. Some trivial shopping errand in the town would send her rushing back to him as if she was returning from a long absence. Her grief-stricken letters, at this time, were in truth love-letters, as poignant as any of her verses.

Her friends had not realized how shattering her loss would be. Except in her verses, she never displayed much emotion; now her anguish was terrible to see. She could not rally, and seemed racked by remorse. An old friend, Eardly Norton, the distinguished Madras barrister, lent her his house, and here she spent the next month, trying to concern herself about a tombstone and the pension to be paid to her child. For his sake she set about completing another volume of poems for which the publishers were waiting. Sometimes, at night, she was seen wandering about the garden of Dunmore House, a living ghost, 'who cut mysterious initials on the bark of many trees', wrote Eardly Norton, later. For whom, for what these initials stood no one has ever disclosed. In the opinion of her friends, she was now unhinged by sorrow. Her last poems, *Indian Love*, are dedicated to her husband in moving lines, written prophetically:

Useless my love—as vain as this regret
That pours my hopeless life across thy grave.

By the time the manuscript reached her publishers, she was dead. On the afternoon of October 4th, two months after her husband's death she killed herself. There were none of the legendary trappings of death in the Orient—of some carved jade poison phial, the thrust of a curved dagger, or the ceremonial of Suttee, the widow's immolation on her husband's funeral pyre. For Laurence Hope, a chemist's packet—perchloride of mercury—achieved this end. They are buried together, in St. Mary's cemetery, Madras.

Once, Hindu widows on their last journey to the funeral pyre, flower-hung and adorned as brides, dipped their hand in a jar of red pigment and on leaving their house, imprinted their mark on the lintel of the door. A few old houses still bear traces of this small, lonely hand bidding farewell to life. Laurence Hope, so steeped in Indian tradition, left no such mark. Only her poems;

> The years go hence, and wild, and lovely things,
> *Their own*, go with them, never to return.